ook, Learn & Create

Bead Jewelry

A WORKSHOP
101
IN A BOOK

Creative Publishing
international

Creative Publishing international

First published in the United States of America by Creative Publishing international, Inc., a member of Quayside Publishing Group
400 First Avenue North
Suite 300
Minneapolis, MN 55401
1-800-328-3895
www.creativepub.com or www.qbookshop.com

Visit www.Craftside.Typepad.com for a behind-the-scenes peek at our crafty world!

ISBN-13: 978-1-58923-665-3
ISBN-10: 1-58923-665-3

10 9 8 7 6 5 4 3 2 1

The Library of Congress has catalogued the earlier edi as follows:

Mitchell, Ann.
  Bead jewelry 101 / by Ann Mitchell and Karen Mitch
    p. cm.
  Includes index
  ISBN 978-1-58923-451-2
  1. Beadwork. 2. Jewerly making. I. Mitchell, Karen
II. Title

  TT860.M58 2009
  745.58'2--dc22

2008053951

Photo Coordinator: Joanne Wawra
Copy Editor: Ellen Goldstein
Cover & Book Design: Mighty Media, Inc.
Page Layout: Mighty Media, Inc.
Videographer: WCK Partners, LLC

CONTENTS

How to Use This Book

So you love jewelry and have always wanted to try your hand at making some yourself. Designing and making beaded jewelry is very appealing and relaxing. But where do you start? If you go to a local bead or craft store, you will find an endless array of parts and beads, so many that it is often difficult to decide what to look at and what tools, beads, and jewelry parts, called findings, you will need. This book will help you understand basic parts and how to use them, and provide you with ideas and instructions to make your own jewelry projects.

First, a photographic glossary shows different findings, tools, beads, and bead accessories with brief descriptions of each item. This visual glossary is followed by a closer look at how to use the basic tools to perform different jewelry-making tasks. Following the initial overview, project chapters are organized by type of finding. There are three projects designed with each finding to teach you, step by step, how to use the featured part in multiple ways to make beautiful pieces of jewelry. At the end of each chapter is a section on variations, presenting you with examples of how simple changes in bead size, shape, color, or pattern can make a big difference in the way the final piece of jewelry looks. Although the projects suggest specific bead choices, feel free to try alternatives—you will find that the variations are unlimited.

Each project is designed to teach you a new technique or basic skill using the finding featured in that chapter. This concept is outlined under **What You'll Learn**.

Quick reference text

Quick reference

A photograph accompanies the **What You'll Need** list so that it will be easy to determine what is necessary to make each design. Tips appear throughout the book to give more detailed suggestions that will help you improve your technique. The Quick References are there to clarify words or phrases printed *like this*. Use this book as a resource for the explanation of different techniques and findings and as a jumping off point for inspiration.

The DVD-ROM included with this book is an additional learning tool that will show you the essential techniques used for making bead jewelry. It is both PC and Mac compatible, and can be viewed using QuickTime software. To download the latest version of QuickTime for free, visit http://www.apple.com/quicktime/download.

As you build your skills, you will be able to expand into making jewelry using multiple findings and techniques in combination. Experiment with the many available options to express yourself creatively. Beaded jewelry has been made and enjoyed for centuries, so have fun learning to make these projects!

The Basics

Making bead jewelry is a very creative, enjoyable craft but, as with most crafts, you can become frustrated if you don't know which tools and materials to buy and how to use them. Manufacturers can't include all the vital information with their packaging, and there are so many options for materials, tools, and techniques. To give you a firm foundation for learning to make bead jewelry, this section teaches you the essentials about tools, findings, accessories, and beads and shows you all of the basic construction techniques you will use for the projects. If you have never tried making jewelry before, you will appreciate the detailed information and photos. Even if you have a little experience making bead jewelry, you are sure to learn some things you didn't know. So settle back, take your time, and explore the basics.

How to Begin

Jewelry making is fun, though with the myriad supplies available, getting started can be confusing or overwhelming. This chapter breaks down how to approach your new interest so that you will enjoy it and not get in over your head with findings and beads before understanding how to organize your ideas and your supplies. You will learn about how to set up a workspace, what tools you will need for most projects, and how to store and organize your supplies. In addition, an outline of design considerations will assist you in choosing your next project.

Where do you start? Before you go to the bead store, think about the space you will be working in. You will need a few basic items:

- A table or other flat surface with enough space to plan your designs
- A comfortable chair at the right height for your worktable
- A light to see what you are working on
- Storage space for beads and findings

Once you have established a work area (which can be portable), you should think about the types of jewelry you would like to make in regard to style and materials. Prior to the bead and findings purchasing trip (to the store or on the Internet), you may want to do a little research by perusing books, magazines, and Web sites for ideas so that you know where you want to start. This book focuses on basic styles constructed with beads of varied sizes and shapes combined with the most commonly used jewelry findings, such as headpins, eye pins, jump rings, beading cable, wire, chain, memory wire, filigree, and additional stringing materials. There is also a chapter on recycling, reusing, and repurposing jewelry parts and beads. The results are attractive, wearable styles that are attainable even to those new to jewelry making. There are also ideas for more advanced jewelry makers. If you are unfamiliar with any of the findings listed, you will find them explained in greater detail in the photographic glossary beginning on page 12.

With a slightly better idea of what you want to make, you will need to purchase a basic set of tools. Here are the most commonly used tools for making bead jewelry, those that you will use for most of the projects in this book:

- Chain-nose pliers—make sure you try them out for the size, shape, and comfort in your hand
- Round-nose pliers

- Wire cutters
- Ruler
- String for measuring necklace, bracelet, and anklet lengths
- Towel, bead mat, or piece of felt to keep beads from rolling on your work surface
- Storage containers for beads and findings

When shopping for tools, purchase good quality items, as you will use them frequently. In addition to this tool selection, there are some other items that will be helpful to you for specific projects:

- Crimp pliers for stringing on beading cable or monofilament
- Scissors, a good all-purpose tool
- Heavy-duty wire cutters for cutting memory wire, which will ruin small cutters
- Bead board with built-in grooves with rulers, compartments for beads, and a flocked surface, which holds beads in place, making necklace and bracelet design much easier

- A second pair of chain-nose pliers, especially helpful for jump ring projects
- Tweezers, which not only are helpful for picking up small beads, but also are very useful for knotting beading thread between beads
- Jump ring tool, which is another good option for closing jump rings
- Knotting tool for knotting thread between beads or as decorative elements on projects

You will need storage boxes. Beads are often small and round and apt to roll into inconvenient places. Choose storage boxes carefully, making sure they have dividers that are fused to the bottom of the box and are not removable. As tempting as it may be to purchase boxes with adjustable compartments, you will be glad later that you did not. Over time the dividers slip, and small beads and parts will sneak into other sections. Unless you really enjoy re-sorting, think twice about adjustable dividers. Also look for

boxes that have grooves in the lid of the box that snap over the dividers so that if the box is closed and gets turned upside down, everything stays in place. As you do more jewelry making, you will find the best way to organize and store your beads and findings in a system that works for you.

Consider storing your beads separately from your findings. You may sort your beads by color, style, or size. Again, you will figure out what works best for you as you start to make more jewelry.

Once you have picked out your workspace and made the initial purchase of tools, you are ready to shop for beads and findings. With an idea of what you plan to make, it is easier to plan a budget for your initial trip to the bead store. If you are not certain of what you will be making, then you may want to set an upper spending limit to start. Let us say that you have selected one of the projects from this book. There is a specific list of supplies and beads you will need for each project, which will make shopping easier and less expensive. The amounts listed will make the design as it is

pictured, so take into account any adjustments you anticipate. If you are purchasing beads randomly to make a variation on a design, you may want to have a few extras for lengthening the design or making matching earrings. Items such as beading wire, crimp beads, clasps, and jump rings can be purchased in larger quantities and used in future projects. Selecting a project from a book, magazine, or Web site is a good way to start, so you'll know exactly what you need. Just make sure that you read through the entire project supply list and instructions before purchasing anything. Once in the bead store, stay focused on your project. Immediately after making your purchases, it is a good idea to sort your findings and beads into storage containers before starting the project.

How do you decide what styles you want to make for yourself? Think about what styles of clothing you wear, the shapes of the necklines, whether you wear more prints or solids, and what length of necklace or earring best suits your body type and the shape of your face. Think about whether you prefer detailed, ornate pieces, bold and chunky accessories, or something simple. All of these factors will help you determine the style of jewelry you will make.

A few design principles and elements that will come into play while you are designing are:

Balance and scale. This relates to the overall balance of the piece, the balance and scale of the individual elements, and the elements as they relate to you and the outfit you are wearing.

Texture and detail. You should determine if you like a lot of texture, small details, or large-scale elements with texture, and whether you like your jewelry smooth, matte, or shiny.

Repetition. You can create visual interest through repetition of color, elements, or patterns.

Color. Think about how your design coordinates with an outfit, how a color or group of colors looks on you, how colors work together, and if you have chosen too many colors for one design.

Comfort and wearability. It is important to consider both the comfort and functionality of a piece of jewelry, and how you can best achieve that without compromising design. Here are a few specifics:
- Earrings. Avoid styles that are noisy or overly heavy.
- Bracelets. Delicate or fragile parts may get knocked off.

- Necklaces. If they are heavy, lumpy, or too long, they could get hooked on countertops or other structures.
- Anklets. If they are too long, they can get caught in sandal straps. You should also avoid beads that make them too lumpy or abrasive.

In addition, necklaces, bracelets, and anklets come in standardized lengths, but may not be the right length for you. Lengths will vary depending on body type, personal preference, neckline, and size of beads and components. The wonderful thing about making your own jewelry is that you can customize it for yourself.

There are many considerations in jewelry design. When people think of jewelry making, often the first picture in their head is of a beaded necklace. So why does this book start with head-pins and other findings, instead of starting with a simple beaded necklace strung on beading wire? Because the techniques learned with the findings form some of the basic elements for earrings and for embellishments on other beaded items. This book presents a progression of findings, and projects that explore their use. The projects in later chapters incorporate the materials and techniques you learned about in earlier chapters. This book will guide you through the basic parts, tools, and techniques for bead jewelry making. The rest is up to you, so have a good time!

Bead sizes

Beads are measured in millimeters. Seed beads are generally sold by weight. Other beads are sold individually or by the strand. Some of the most common sizes for glass and gemstone beads are 2mm, 4mm, 6mm, 8mm, 10mm, and 12mm. For larger quantities, beads are sold by the mass, which consists of 1200 beads.

Size	Number of beads on a 16" or 400mm strand	Bead Sizes	Diameter
2mm	203	15/0 Seed bead	1.3mm
4mm	100	11/0 Seed bead	1.8mm
6mm	67	8/0 Seed bead	2.5mm
8mm	50	6/0 Seed bead	3.3mm
10mm	41	e-bead	4mm

Photographic Glossary

In this section, many of the materials you will encounter while crafting beaded jewelry are listed alphabetically under these headings: Tools, Findings, Accessories, and Beads. Look to this section for detailed descriptions and photographs of materials.

Tools

BEAD BOARDS

Bead boards are flat and have graduated calibrated beading channels and recessed storage areas. Used to lay out and plan bead designs and organize beads and findings, most boards are flocked to prevent objects from rolling.

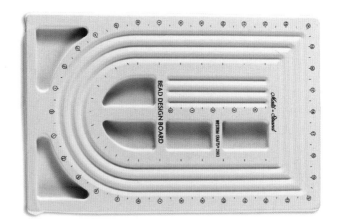

BEADING NEEDLES

Beading needles are available in flexible wire or stiff metal and used to guide beads onto a bead cord that does not come with an attached needle. Use collapsible eye needles with beads that have very small holes.

BEAD REAMERS

Bead reamers have long diamond grit covered tips, are used for enlarging and smoothing out holes in beads. Also available in a battery-operated version.

JUMP RING TOOL

Jump ring tool is a ring designed to fit over a finger with two different sized slots on top. Jump rings can be fitted into one of the slots and the tool is twisted to open and close the jump rings. Slots are different sizes to accommodate various sizes of jump rings.

KNOTTING TOOL

Knotting tool has a pin with a Y-shaped prong next to it and is used to form tight knots between beads strung on silk or nylon bead cord.

PLIERS AND WIRE CUTTERS

Pliers and wire cutters are each designed for a special purpose.

Chain-nose pliers, also known as flat nose pliers, have a fine nose with double half-round tips and are used to form loops and other configurations in wire, close bead tips, open and close jump rings, flatten crimps, and attach findings. The flat interior of the nose will not mar wire if used gently.

Crimp pliers are used to close and secure crimp beads and tubes. The inner position on the pliers forms a groove and the outer position rounds the crimp, making it smooth and comfortable. Pliers are available in different sizes to coordinate with different sizes of crimp tubes.

Nylon-tipped, flat-jawed pliers are used to help shape coated wire without marking the wire. They are also used to straighten wire before use by lightly pulling the wire through the pliers.

Tools continued

Round-nose pliers, tapered and slim with double-round tips, are used for looping and shaping wire into curves. Combination flat/round tipped pliers are also available for making sharp bends in wire, uniform loops, and jump rings.

Split ring pliers have one straight tip and one tip with a small hook on the end. They are used to separate split rings and keep them separated in order to attach other findings.

Heavy-duty wire cutters cut heavy wire gauges and steel wire such as memory wire. Memory wire can also be cut with memory wire shears.

Wire cutters are used to cut beading wires, small gauge wires, coated wire, and other soft wire. These cutters are not for use on heavy gauge wire or memory wire.

STORAGE CONTAINERS

Storage containers in which
to store beads and findings
are available in many types.
Boxes with sections work
well—look for those with
attached dividers and lids
that close snugly over the
sections in order to avoid
accidental mixing of beads
and parts.

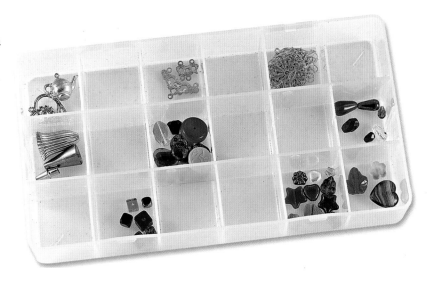

STRAIGHT TWEEZERS

Straight tweezers with long narrow tapered tips
are used to help slide knots snugly next to each
bead strung on silk or nylon bead cord. Tweezers
can also be used to pick up small beads and
crimp beads.

WIRE JIG

Wire jig has a metal or plastic base with evenly
spaced holes. Pegs of different sizes are placed
in the holes to form a pattern and wire is wound
around the pegs to make a loop or finding to be
used in a jewelry design.

WORK SURFACES

Work surfaces are bead mats made of foam to keep
beads and findings from rolling around. Towels or
felt pieces can also be used as work surfaces.

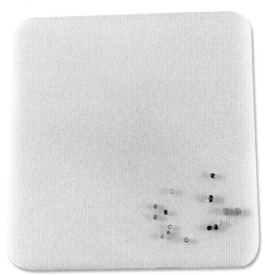

Findings

"Findings" is a generic term for components used to assemble jewelry.

BAILS

Bails made of metal are attached to a bead then clipped or slid onto chain or cord to form a pendant attachment. Pinch bails fold over to form the attachment loop for the chain and can be squeezed together so that the pointed ends on each end of the bail fit into holes of a tip-drilled or side-drilled bead.

BARRETTES

Barrettes are flat metal hair clip bases that are available in a number of sizes up to four inches (10 cm). French made clips are superior in quality.

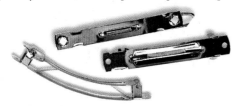

BEAD CORD

Bead cord is thin cord of silk or nylon designed specifically for stringing beads. Short lengths are available with an attached needle. Often used to string beads with knots in between, different diameter cord is used for different sizes of beads.

BEADING CABLE OR FLEXIBLE BEADING WIRE

Beading cable or flexible beading wire is composed of tiny metal wires that are twisted together and coated with nylon. The greater the number of strands, the more flexible the cable. Beading cable is available in different diameters; smaller diameters are appropriate for smaller beads, peyote stitch, and bead weaving, and large heavier beads require larger diameter wire. There are also a variety of metals and colors available.

CELL PHONE STRAPS

Cell phone straps are thin straps with a loop on the end which can be attached through the hole on a cell phone or PDA. An assortment of decorative elements can be attached to the loop.

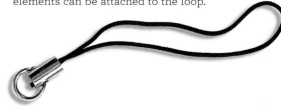

CHAINS

Chains consist of a series of joined loops and/or connectors. Some of the types of chains available are as follows:

Bar chain has flat, round or decorative bars connected with small loops.

Cable chain consists of all the same size loops where every other link interlocks perpendicular to the next link.

Curb chain has same-size loops that interlock and twist so that all the loops are parallel to each other and the chain lies flat.

Figaro chain is made in a pattern of a smaller oval loop or loops followed by a larger loop.

Loop and connector chain has flat connectors between the loops.

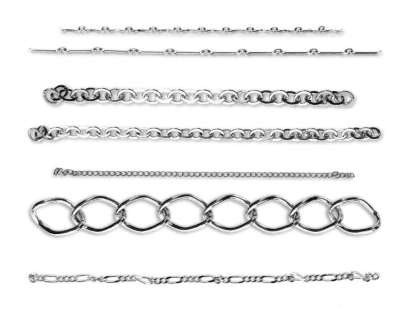

CHOKER CLAMPS OR RIBBON CLAMPS

Choker clamps or ribbon clamps are fold-over rectangular flat clamps that can be squeezed together around a ribbon end, finishing the end. Clasps or other findings can be attached to the loop on the clamp. Clamps have grips to hold the ribbon, but should be glued as well.

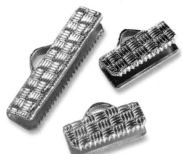

CLAMSHELL ENDS

Clamshell ends are similar in shape to a clam and can be placed over the knot at the end of strung bead cord or silk. Use chain nose pliers to close the clamshell over the knot, covering it. The attached loop on the clamshell end can be used to attach a clasp or other jewelry findings.

CLASPS

Clasps come in a wide range of styles:

Barrel or torpedo shaped clasps have two sides that screw together. Loops on the ends of the clasp components spin freely, allowing the two sides to be screwed together without twisting the jewelry piece.

Box and tongue or filigree (pearl) clasps have a flat folded side or tongue that fits into a box-shaped side. The tongue side acts as a spring that holds the two sides together. These clasps are available with various numbers of attached loops for creating multi-strand designs. A pearl clasp has a tongue that hooks as well for added safety.

Decorative clasps are fancy versions of box and tongue clasps and function in a similar manner. They are available decorated with pearls, beads, or rhinestones, or an unadorned finding to which decorative elements can be added.

Fold over clasps have a loop on one side and a flat hook on the other side. The hook passes through the loop and then folds back on itself to close.

Friction clasps consist of two curved metal tubes that slide into one another and are held together by friction.
The ends can be crimped, glued, or soldered onto beading wire or chain.

Lobster clasps are shaped like a lobster's claw with a spring-operated pincer. The lobster clasp is easy to operate and reliable.

Magnetic clasps have a very small but powerful magnet in each side that holds the clasp closed. Magnetic clasps work well for individuals that have difficulty operating other types of clasps.

S hook or hook and eye clasps have a hook finding on one end and a loop on the other.

Slide clasps are multi-strand clasps that consist of two parts of a bar with loops on one side and a tube with loops on the other side. The sides slide together and are held by a spring friction mechanism.

Spring ring clasps are round clasps with a spring-operated lever that pulls back to open.

Toggle clasps have a bar on one side and a large and often decorative ring on the other. To attach, slide the bar through the ring.

COIL ENDS OR SPRING CORD ENDS

Coil ends or spring cord ends are made of coiled steel wire with a loop and used over the end of leather, rubber, satin, or velour cord. The ends are glued on for security.

COLORED CRAFT WIRE

Colored craft wire is permanently colored copper wire or copper wire covered in colored plastic. This wire is generally used to make decorative elements.

CORD

Cord refers to any type of flexible material used for stringing beads or hanging pendants, usually a dimensional material such as real or imitation leather or suede lace, ribbon, rubber cording, satin cording, velour tubing, or hemp.

CRIMP BEADS OR TUBES

Crimp beads or tubes are small metal tubes; the beads are rounded on the edges and crimp tubes are cylindrical. They are pressed or flattened in over beading cable to finish the ends and hold beads in place. Both crimp beads and tubes are available in a variety of hole diameters and lengths.

EARRING FINDINGS

Earring findings come in several varieties.

Clip-ons are made for individuals with non-pierced ears. They are available in several configurations used for both dangle and post style earrings. Dangle styles consist of ball, stick, or decorative designs for the front of the ear and flip, screw, or a combination closure for the back and include a loop for a dangle. Post clip-on earring findings vary in pad size to attach to different size earrings and may include a loop for a dangle.

Cup pad posts have a cupped pad or cupped pad with a peg for attaching a round earring top, or a half drilled round top.

Flat pad posts are posts with a flat pad on which to attach the decorative part of the earring. These are for earrings that sit on the ear lobe, or for the top of an earring that also has a dangle.

French ear wires, ball and coil ear wires, or ball and spring ear wires are hooks that slip through the ear and have no closure. They can be secured with a rubber French wire keeper.

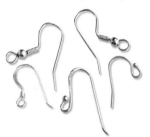

French wire keepers are small rubber or plastic cylinders that slide snugly onto the backs of French earring wires to keep them from slipping out of the ear.

Hoops are continuous or partial loops, some with built-in posts, usually round in shape. Some hoops are available as a complete finding to which drops can be added.

Kidney wires are kidney-shaped pierced earring wires that have a hook in the back to hold the end of the wire.

Lever-back wires have hinged backs that close completely at the back of the ear. They can have a plain or decorative front.

Nuts are post backs that grip the back of the earring to hold it in place. Small standard nuts are called butterfly nuts, larger mechanical grip nuts are considered more secure and are available with or without a plastic flange. Nuts with a plastic disk or flange are used to keep large earrings that sit on the earlobe from drooping or hanging awkwardly on the ear.

Posts are earring findings with a ball, half ball, or decorative element at the top and a loop on which to attach a dangle.

Threaders are made with very fine chain and have an attached post on one end and some type of loop or decorative element on the other. The post and part of the chain is pulled through the ear.

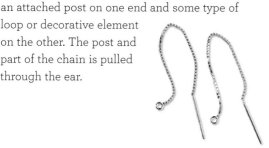

ELASTIC

Elastic for beading is a UV resistant stretch cord specifically designed for jewelry applications and is available in different diameters.

EYEGLASS LEASH ENDS

Eyeglass leash ends are available in a double loop or ball and loop style and are attached to both ends of an eyeglass leash. The loops are made from rubber to slip over and hold securely onto the temples of eyeglasses.

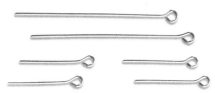

EYE PINS

Eye pins are straight wire jewelry findings with a loop on one end. Available in a variety of diameters, lengths, and metals, they are used as connecting elements in jewelry design and are often used with beads.

FILIGREES

Filigrees are made of stamped metal and available in many different styles. Drops can be added to make chandelier earrings, filigree pieces can be attached together with jump rings or used as spacers for bracelets or necklaces, or a pin back can be attached to the back to make a brooch.

HEADPINS

Headpins are straight wire jewelry findings with a flat head on one end often used for making beaded drops. They are available with decorative heads or set crystal heads, and can be found in a variety of diameters, lengths, and metals.

GLUE

Glue is any of an assortment of products used to adhere jewelry findings:

Cyanoacrylate is a super glue that bonds metal, plastic, and glass.

Epoxy is a two-part adhesive that requires mixing and usually has a specific usability window and drying time.

E-6000 is clear, flexible, and waterproof and good for gluing metal and plastic.

G-S Hypo Cement is a precision applicator glue, not for use on metal-to-metal but good for gluing elastic and monofilament.

JUMP RINGS

Jump rings are metal loops with a single opening. Used to attach clasps, findings, or different jewelry elements together, they come in many different metals, platings, sizes, and gauges. If you plan to manipulate the rings by hand, choose a thickness that can be opened and closed easily without bending the loop out of shape.

MEMORY WIRE

Memory wire is thin, tempered, stainless steel wire that is formed into a spring and sized for rings, bracelets, anklets, and chokers. Memory wire should be cut with heavy-duty cutters or shears, and any number of loops can be cut for a design. Ends can be coiled using round nose pliers or finished with memory wire ends.

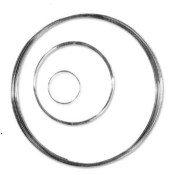

MONOFILAMENT

Monofilament is a non-elastic, clear nylon stringing material. Generally used for "floating" necklaces, where beads are crimped or glued onto the monofilament with some nylon left exposed between the beads.

PADS WITH LOOPS OR DISKS WITH BAILS

Pads with loops or disks with bails are small metal pads with attached loops. They can be glued onto the back of pendants, filigree, or flat back stones, providing a loop to help incorporate that element into a jewelry design. Disks with bails have a larger pad and can be used in the same way.

PIN BACKS OR BAR PINS

Pin backs or bar pins can be glued or soldered onto the back of a jewelry element to make a brooch.

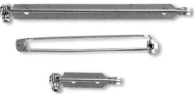

SOLID RINGS OR LINKS

Solid rings or links are made of soldered metal or stone, shell, plastic or other material and can be attached with jump rings to form a link or other decorative element in a design.

SPLIT RINGS

Split rings are loops made of tempered wire styled like a miniature key ring. These are easiest to open using split ring pliers and they provide a very secure attachment for findings.

WAXED LINEN

Waxed linen thread is used to string beads. Designs made with waxed linen often have beads with a knot on each side and a length of thread left exposed between the beads as a design element.

WIRE

Wire is a pliable strand of metal that is available in a variety of gauges and metals. The smaller the gauge number, the larger the diameter of the wire. Wire can be used in lieu of head pins or eye pins to form findings for bead drops or segments. It can also be formed into decorative design elements using pliers or a jig.

WIRELACE™

WireLace™ is tubular metallic mesh ribbon of brass, copper, or aluminum, available in several widths and colors. Use it as a decorative element or stringing material.

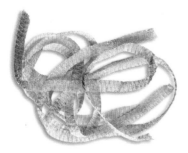

Accessories

BEAD CAPS

Bead caps are decorative concave disk components with a hole in the center and are used on one or both sides of a bead to embellish the overall design. Different sizes of bead caps are available for different bead sizes. A variety of looks can be obtained by using the same size cap on different sizes of beads. There are also bell caps, which have a loop at the top to accommodate beads or stones that do not have through-holes, so the bead or stone must be glued in place to make a drop or charm.

CHARMS

Charms are cast or stamped metal parts with a loop representing myriad shapes and themes.

CONE ENDS

Cone ends have holes in both ends and are used to finish the ends of a multi-strand necklace neatly. They can also be used as tassel tops or large bead caps.

MULTI-STRAND END BARS

Multi-strand end bars have a flat bar, usually metal, that generally has a single loop on one side and multiple loops on the other side. End bars are often decorative and are used to keep strands aligned and untangled on multi-strand necklaces. They can also be used as earring components to create multi-drop styles.

RHINESTONE RONDELLES

Rhinestone rondelles consist of pointed-back rhinestones channel set between two metal disks with a center hole from top to bottom. They are placed between beads as embellishment. There are a variety of sizes to accommodate different bead sizes. They also come in a square version, called squaredelles.

SPACERS

Spacers are flat beads of metal, glass, plastic, or shell that are used between other beads in a strand or on earrings to add visual interest. Flat spacers can be used in multiples to create texture.

SPACER BARS

Spacer bars are thin bars with multiple holes that are used to hold multiple strands of beads in alignment, usually on a bracelet or necklace. The number of holes corresponds to the number of strands on the piece, and the distances between the holes on the spacer bars are designed to accommodate different sizes of beads.

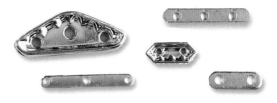

TINY BEADS AND SEED BEADS

Tiny beads and seed beads 2mm or 3mm of metal, metallic plastic, or glass are used between other beads in a strand or earrings as an enhancement. Tiny beads can be used to simulate knots between beads.

Beads

Bead Materials

Beads are available in an infinite variety of types, colors, materials, and finishes. This glossary gives you an overview of the materials beads can be made from and some of their shapes and finishes. It can help you identify beads that you may want to use for your designs.

BONE AND HORN BEADS

Bone and horn beads are carved from the bones or horns of yak, camel, or water buffalo.

CERAMIC BEADS

Ceramic beads are made from ceramic material or porcelain, can be glazed, textured, shaped, or painted.

CRYSTAL BEADS

Crystal beads are of high quality glass that contains more than 10% lead oxide; top-quality Austrian crystal contains 32%. Beads are machine cut and polished. Crystal can also refer to beads made from natural rock crystal.

GLASS BEADS

Glass beads come in myriad of shapes and sizes.

African trade beads are made from fused powdered glass and have a grainy matte appearance. They are often decorated with various patterns.

Czech druk are smooth round glass beads.

Czech fire-polished beads are machine faceted glass beads that are polished in a hot oven, which melts the facets slightly and rounds the edges. They are available in a number of glass finishes.

Czech pressed glass beads are pressed into a variety of shapes.

Czech table cut beads are mold-shaped beads with flat cut fronts and backs.

Dichroic beads have thin layers of metallic oxides deposited on the glass by a vacuum furnace. This gives the glass a fiery iridescence.

e-beads are glass seed beads that are cut from a long tube of glass. Beads are slightly flattened on the sides instead of being perfectly round.

Fiber-optic beads are made from glass fibers that are fused and then cut by machine. They have a unique sheen and cannot be made in red. Miracle beads are manufactured in a similar manner using granules.

Furnace glass is heated in a furnace and shaped by hand from long canes of glass.

India glass comes in a variety of shapes and textures produced in India using Czech and Italian techniques.

Lampwork glass beads are made using a flame to melt the glass. An artist winds the molten glass around a steel mandrel, textures the bead with various tools and embellishes by adding color.

Murano or Italian glass beads are made in Italy with historic techniques. Fiorato beads have layered glass embellishments in the shape of flowers; millefiore beads are made from glass canes that are layered and cut. The Italians also produce hand blown hollow beads.

Seed beads are small smooth glass beads often used for bead weaving on a loom and complex stringing designs. Seed beads are mostly round, though some square shapes are available, and they come in a variety of sizes.

METAL BEADS

Metal beads are made from a variety of metals.

Cloisonné beads have attached metal wire that forms patterns or cloisons, which are filled with glass enamel and then fired.

Metal beads can be machined or cast out of a variety of different metals including precious metals. Some precious metal beads are laser or diamond cut for texture.

Metallized plastic beads are molded plastic beads with metal plating.

Thai silver beads have a textured silver exterior with a resin center.

PEARLS

Pearls are cultured in fresh or salt water. Synthetic varieties are also available.

Freshwater pearls of different shapes and sizes are formed in a farmed freshwater mollusk that has had a "seed" or starter shape placed inside. Some colors are achieved by dyeing, others by radiation. Natural colors range from cream white to peach and pink.

Cultured pearls, created by introducing a "seed" into a saltwater oyster, are considered higher in quality than freshwater pearls due to the deeper luster of the nacre coating. Natural pearls are created when a bit of sand gets inside the shell of wild oysters and is then coated with nacre; these pearls are usually round.

Faux pearls are made with a pearlized synthetic coating over a crystal, glass, or plastic base.

PLASTIC BEADS

Plastic beads come in several types and many shapes and sizes. Plastic offers a lighter weight option for jewelry designs.

Bakelite plastic was developed in the early 1900s. It was molded, carved, and extruded into jewelry parts.

Lucite was developed and popularized in the 1930s. Lucite is a crystal clear plastic that is also known as acrylic, acrylic resin, or plexiglass. Beads were generally carved from a tube.

Generic plastic can be molded into a huge variety of shapes and sizes of beads. It can also be printed with patterns.

RESIN

Resin can be used to make beads. Organic resin is a plant secretion often used in adhesives and varnishes. Resin beads are generally made from synthetic resin, and can be made to imitate stone, sea glass, or cinnabar.

POLYMER CLAY

Polymer clay is a lightweight modeling material that can be cured in a regular oven. Polymer clay can be used to imitate many types of beads including glass and stone. They are most commonly available for purchase as "caned" beads with patterns similar to Italian millefiore.

SHELL

Shell beads can be made with an entire shell or cut and shaped, and are available in natural colors or dyed varieties. Heishi shell beads are cut from ostrich eggshells or mollusk shells.

STONE

Stone beads, often referred to as semi-precious or gemstone beads, are cut and shaped from natural stones. They can be enhanced by dye, heat treatment, or irradiation or coated with resin or wax. Some stones, such as cherry quartz, are actually manmade.

WOOD AND NUT BEADS

Wood and nut beads, cut and shaped from a variety of woods and nuts, can be dyed, textured, carved, or painted.

Bead Finishes

AURORA BOREALIS

Aurora Borealis, or AB, is a multicolored rainbow finish on the outside of a bead, often on only one side.

GHOST

Ghost is a matte bead with an aurora borealis finish.

IRIS

Iris is an all over iridescent finish on a dark opaque bead.

LUSTER

Luster is a type of reflective finish on a translucent bead.

MATTE

Matte is a frosted finish.

OPAL

Opal is slightly milky, somewhat transparent glass.

OPAQUE

Opaque is non-translucent; no light passes through it.

SPECIALTY COATING

Specialty coating can be multicolored, stone-like, or pearlized. Glass beads can be dipped and fired using a variety of types of coatings.

TRANSLUCENT

Translucent or transparent beads let the light shine through.

Bead Shapes

BICONE

BRIOLETTE

BUTTON

CHIPS

COIN

CONE

CUBE

DAGGER

DROP

LENTIL

NUGGET

OVAL

POTATO

RECTANGLE

RICE

RONDELLE

ROUND

ROUND FACET

SHAPED

TRIANGLE

TUBE

Construction Techniques

This chapter outlines some basic jewelry-making techniques that you will use repeatedly. All of these techniques are explored in the projects of the following chapters, and have been consolidated here for the purpose of quick reference.

MAKING WIRE LOOPS

There are a variety of ways to form a wire loop in jewelry making. Round-nose pliers can be used in combination with chain-nose pliers or chain-nose pliers can be used alone. Many of the projects in this book use chain-nose pliers. Please use what works best for you.

Making a Loop Using Chain-nose Pliers

1 Hold the stacked beads between your thumb and fingers, keeping all the beads stacked closely together and touching the flat base of the headpin. Use chain-nose pliers to bend the wire at a 90-degree angle just above the top bead.

2 Using chain-nose pliers, form a ⅛" (3 mm) loop by bending the headpin wire in the opposite direction of the first bend.

3 Trim the excess wire from the loop with your wire cutters so that it will be even once it is closed.

Making a Loop Using Round-nose Pliers

1 Use chain-nose pliers to bend the wire at a 90-degree angle just above the top bead.

2 Cut off any excess beyond about ⅜" (1 cm) (less for a smaller loop).

3 Grasp the end of the wire with round-nose pliers and roll the wire around the pliers, forming a loop. Using a different location on the jaws of the round-nose pliers will vary the size of the loop. For consistent size loops for any given project, mark the preferred loop size spot on the jaws of the pliers with a permanent marker.

Making a Wrapped Loop

1 Use chain-nose pliers to bend the wire at a 90-degree angle about ⅛" (3 mm) above the top bead. Leave at least 1" (2.5 cm) of wire above the bend.

2 Form a loop above the bend using round-nose pliers. If attaching the drop to a chain with soldered loops, hook the drop onto the chain before wrapping the loop.

3 Grasp the loop with chain-nose pliers in one hand, and with your other hand wrap the tail end of the wire or headpin back around the stem several times below the loop.

4 Trim the excess with wire cutters.

 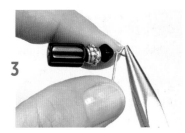

TIP Wrapped loops are easier to do with thinner head or eye pins, or with wire off a spool. It is difficult to wrap wire neatly if it is too thick.

HOW TO MAKE A DROP WITH A HEADPIN

1 Slide the hole of a bead over the wire and then slide the bead down to sit snugly against the flat or decorative head of the headpin.

2 Once the selected number of beads has been added to the headpin, form a loop on the wire and clip off the excess.

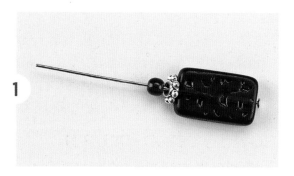

HOW TO OPEN THE LOOP ON AN EARRING HOOK

Many types of earring findings have a loop at the bottom to attach the earring. Many of these have a split in the loop so that it can be opened and closed. When an earring drop has a wrapped loop at the top or a finding has a cast loop, it is necessary to open the loop on the earring hook in order to attach the drop or finding.

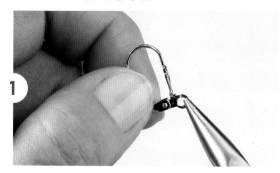

1 Hold the earring hook in one hand and grasp the loop with chain-nose pliers. Open the loop by gently bending it perpendicular to the direction of the loop. Do not pull the loop open parallel to the loop because it will be very difficult to line up and close.

2 Once the drop or finding has been slipped over the earring hook loop, close the loop in the opposite direction with the chain-nose pliers.

OPENING AND CLOSING A JUMP RING

1 Hold the jump ring next to the cut in the ring with a pair of chain-nose pliers. Hold the opposite side of the jump ring with another pair of chain-nose pliers or your fingers.

2 Once the jump ring has been looped through the finding it is being attached to, bring the ends of the jump ring back together in the same manner by keeping the ends *perpendicular* to the ring. Make sure the cut ends are flush with no gap.

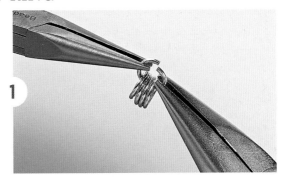

Using the Jump Ring Tool

Jump rings can also be opened and closed using a jump ring tool. Slide the tool onto your index finger, slide the jump ring into one of the slots in the tool, and twist gently to open jump ring. Slots are different widths to accommodate different jump ring sizes.

HOW TO USE AN EYE PIN

To use an eye pin to make a link or drop, slide the hole of the bead over the end of the wire, until the bead sits snugly next to the eye of the pin. Once the selected number of beads is added, form a loop on the wire end and cut off the excess.

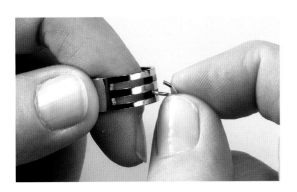

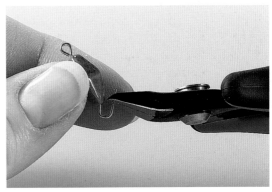

USING SPLIT RING PLIERS

Split rings are loops made of tempered wire styled like a miniature key ring. They provide a very secure attachment for findings. It is easiest to open split rings using split ring pliers. Insert the curved nose of the pliers between the loops of the split ring and press down on the handles to push the nose of the pliers together. This will hold the split ring open to attach it to other findings.

ADDING A CLASP

1 Open a 6.5mm jump ring by bending the ends away from each other perpendicular to the ring (you can vary the jump ring size depending on the scale of the piece you are finishing).

2 Hook the jump ring through one end of the chain or end loop you are adding the clasp to.

3 Close the jump ring, aligning the ends so that there is no space between them.

4 Open a 4mm jump ring and hook it through the other end of the chain. Attach the clasp to the jump ring and close the ring.

TIP Some necklace designs have a front side and a back side. Depending on whether you are right-handed or left-handed, put the clasp on the end of the necklace you prefer, making sure the design is right side up.

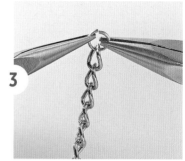

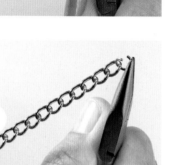

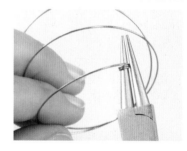

MAKING AN END LOOP ON MEMORY WIRE

Grasp the end of the memory wire with round-nose pliers, positioning the pliers according to the size of loop you want. Use the pliers to form a double loop. Make sure that the cut end does not protrude so it will not scratch the wearer.

MEASURING A BRACELET LENGTH

When measuring your wrist size to determine bracelet length, remember to include the length of the type of clasp you are using. Make the bracelet long enough so that you can close the clasp yourself, but not so long that it will slide over your hand while the clasp is shut. Generally, a comfortable bracelet measurement is 1" (2.5 cm) longer than your wrist measurement. A bit more may be added to accommodate larger beads.

HOW TO USE CRIMP PLIERS AND CRIMP BEADS/TUBES

Crimp tubes, beads, or slides provide a quick and neat way to finish a piece of jewelry strung on beading cable or monofilament.

1 Slide the crimp tube or bead onto the beading cable after the final bead has been added.

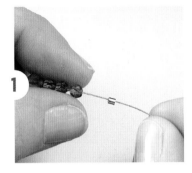

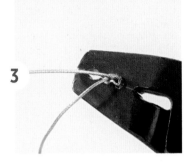

2 String the beading cable through the jump ring or other finding to which the element is to be attached. Run the cable back through the crimp; the cable can also be run through a bead or several beads next to the crimp.

3 Pull the beading cable tight, leaving a sufficient amount of wire to allow for the proper movement of the necklace or jewelry element. Note: To show proper placement, the cable has not been pulled tight on the photo. Using crimp pliers, place the crimp in the inner position of the pliers

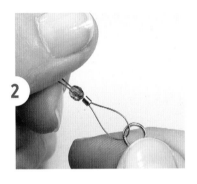

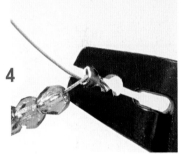

located closest to the hinge in the handle. Press down on the crimp pliers to make a groove in the tube or bead.

4 Move the crimp to the outer position of the pliers, closest to the nose. Press down on the

pliers and the crimp will round out. Crimp beads or tubes can be pressed flat with chain-nose pliers, though sometimes this leaves a sharp corner, which may be uncomfortable for the wearer.

TIP If a necklace features a center drop with an odd number of beaded drops, you will want to have an odd number of loops in the length of chain that you cut. You may need to adjust the length of the chain to end up with an odd number of loops.

MEASURING A NECKLACE LENGTH

Drape a piece of string around your neck at the place where you would like your necklace to hang. Measure the string to determine the length of chain you will need. Cut the chain to the measured length of the string using cutters.

Beaded drops add weight to the chain, so the necklace will hang a bit lower than a piece of string of the same length. Also, the clasp and loops at the back closure will add about ⅝" (1.6 cm) to the finished length.

BASIC KNOTTING

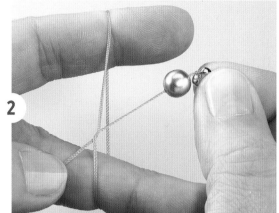

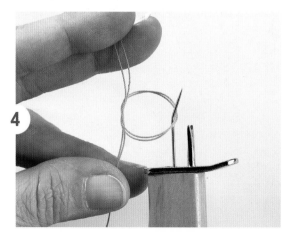

1 Cut a piece of thread four times the length of the jewelry piece you are making. Thread it through a beading needle, bringing the ends of the thread together. Tie an overhand knot at the end of the two strands. Tie a second overhand knot over the first one, enlarging the knot. Slide a clamshell end over the strands to cover the knot.

2 Slide on the first bead. With your left hand, if you are right handed, make a "V" with your index and middle finger; the middle finger should be closer to your palm. Holding the end of the thread with your right hand, wrap the thread away from you around your index finger and then your middle finger, and bring it around to the side facing you. Drop the bead over the wrapped thread into the loop you have formed around your fingers.

3 Point the tip of the awl on the knotting tool through the loop from left to right and wrap the thread halfway around it.

4 Slide the thread loop off of your fingers and onto the awl portion of the knotting tool.

5 Pull the thread so that it tightens around the awl and also so that the knot slides toward the bead.

6 Turn the tool in your right hand, reversing the position of the awl end and Y prong. Place the thread into the Y prong on the knotting tool and pull the thread tight. Keep your left index finger on the top portion of the knotting tool so that the thread does not slide off the tip until you want it to. Carefully slide the knot toward the top of the awl, and onto the bent tip. Keeping the tension in the thread through the Y prong, use your right thumb to push up on the spring-loaded metal top of the tool. This will slide the knot off of the awl and tighten the knot next to the bead. Slide the next bead onto the thread, and repeat the knotting technique. Keep adding beads and knotting.

7 Make a knot after the last bead. Slide on the second clamshell, with the shell portion facing away from the beads. Use the knotting tool to make a knot inside the clamshell, and then repeat a second time.

8 Trim excess thread and use chain-nose pliers to close the clamshell. Bend the end prong into a closed loop. Trim the excess thread and close the clamshell on the other end of the bracelet. To one clamshell loop, hook on a 4.5mm jump ring and the clasp, then close the jump ring. Open a 6mm jump ring and attach it to the other clamshell loop. Close the jump ring.

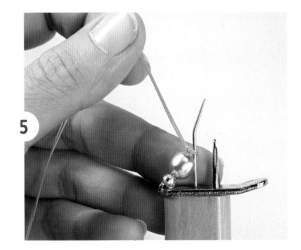

5

6

7

8

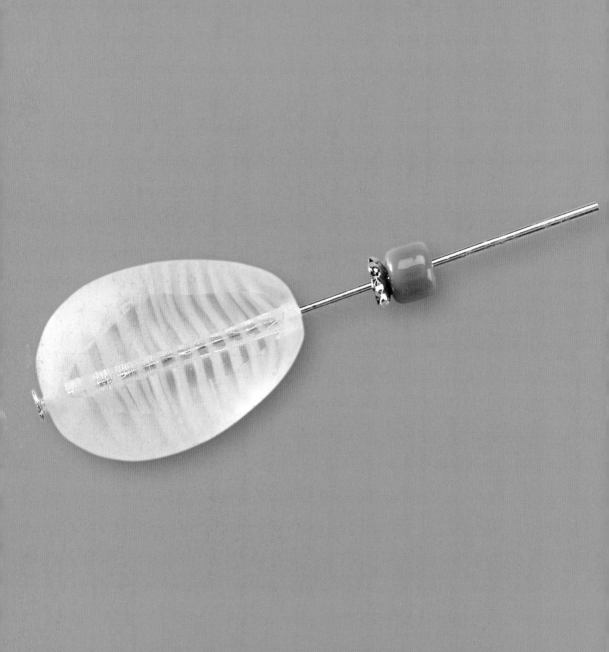

The Projects

The projects in this section are organized by the type of finding used to make the jewelry pieces. For each finding, there are three projects that incorporate the featured finding in different ways. While you probably will not make all the projects in order, it is well worth your time to read through all the projects and study the techniques introduced in each one. Specific materials used for each project are listed and shown in a photograph to help you make selections. Feel free to substitute similar bead alternatives—personalizing your jewelry is what this craft is all about. We have included many variations of the project pieces to inspire you to think of more creative ways to apply the techniques you have learned.

HEADPINS:
Basic Drop Earrings

Headpins play an important role in beaded jewelry design. Drops made with headpins and beads can be used individually to make simple, elegant earrings or a Y-necklace pendant. Combining drops on filigree, chain, or a beaded strand creates endless options for charm bracelets, chandelier earrings, multi-drop necklaces, or other types of accessory designs. Headpins are available in a variety of different metals, different colored platings, and many lengths.

WHAT YOU'LL LEARN..

- Basic technique to make drops for a broad range of jewelry designs
- The importance of proportion and balance for a simple drop earring
- How to use a spacer bead for interest
- How to attach a drop to an earring hook

WHAT YOU'LL NEED..

TOOLS

- Chain-nose pliers
- Wire cutters

MATERIALS

- Two $7/16$" × $1 1/16$" (4mm × 2.6cm) cobalt rectangular pressed glass beads
- Two small antique silver-tone spacers
- Two 4mm cobalt Czech druk beads
- Two 2" (5 cm) silver-tone headpins
- Two silver-tone French ear wires

How to Make Basic Drop Earrings

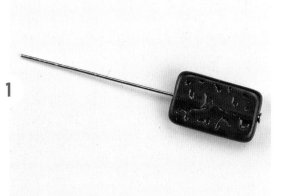

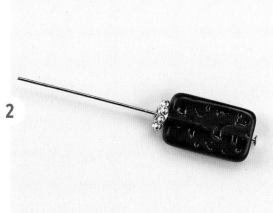

1 Slide a cobalt rectangular bead onto one head-pin so that it touches the base of the headpin.

2 Slide an antique silver spacer so that it sits directly on top of the rectangular bead.

3 Add the 4mm cobalt druk bead and slide it down to rest on the spacer.

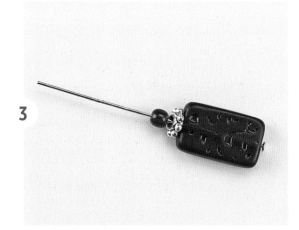

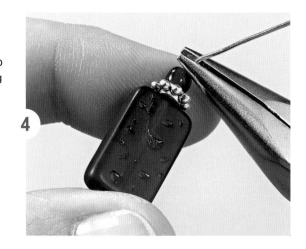

4 Hold the **stacked beads** between your thumb and fingers; keeping all the beads stacked closely together touching the flat base of the headpin. Use your chain-nose pliers to bend the wire at a 90-degree angle just above the top of the druk bead.

TIP When working with glass, crystal, and stone beads, be careful not to bend the wire too close to the top of the bead, as you may chip it. Try sliding the pliers so that the bottom edge is slightly (less than 1/16" [1.6mm]) above the bead before bending the wire at a right angle, making sure not to apply pressure on the bead hole with the wire while bending.

5 Use either your chain-nose or your round-nose pliers to form a ⅛" (3mm) loop by bending the headpin wire in the opposite direction of the first bend.

6 ***Trim the loop*** so that it will be even once it is closed.

7 Hook the open loop through the loop on the bottom of the ear wire, and then close the loop using your pliers.

8 Repeat all steps to make the matching earring.

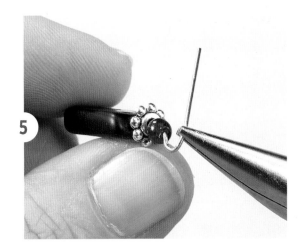

QUICK REFERENCE

Stacked beads. It is not necessary to use separators, rondelles, or smaller beads between the featured beads on your drop, but they will help define the main beads, especially if they are the same color.

Trim the loop. If you plan your design in advance, select the shortest possible headpin that will allow for the size loop you plan to make on the drop. This will reduce the amount of wire waste when you clip off the excess. This is especially important if you are using precious metal headpins.

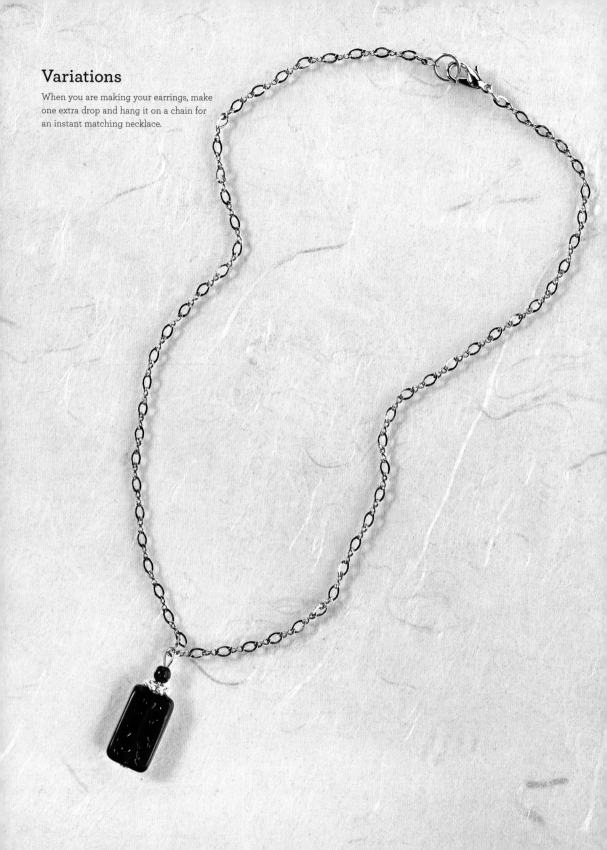

Variations

When you are making your earrings, make
one extra drop and hang it on a chain for
an instant matching necklace.

Vary the size of the beads, metal color, and spacers to create a completely different style.

Create a delicate, elongated drop earring by using all the same size bead on the headpin, accented with metallic seed beads between. You can vary the length by changing the number of beads.

Shift the balance of the beads by putting the larger ones on top and the smaller ones on the bottom, and the look will change completely.

HEADPINS:
Multi-drop Necklace

You have gained an understanding of the easiest way to add beads to a headpin and use it in a simple design. Now the fun really begins as you start to experiment with some more creative construction using the same simple beaded headpin elements. With a minor variation in bead shape, you can add subtle texture and interest to a multi-drop necklace. The repetition of the drops creates visual impact for a simple yet dramatic necklace.

WHAT YOU'LL LEARN . . . .

- How to vary bead shapes on your drops to add texture to a design
- How to add caps to drops for a subtle accent
- How to use repetition as a design element

WHAT YOU'LL NEED . . . .

TOOLS

- One 30" (76.2 cm) piece of string to measure necklace length
- Chain-nose or round-nose pliers
- Wire cutters
- Ruler

MATERIALS

- 16" to 20" (40.6 to 50.8 cm) silver-tone medium round loop link and connector chain (⅜" [1 cm] loops)

- Five 12 × 18mm table-cut teardrop glass beads: lime green stripe
- Six 12 × 14mm table-cut rounded rectangular glass beads: lime green stripe
- Eleven e-beads: opaque lime green
- Eleven 4mm silver-tone bead caps
- One 6.5mm silver-tone jump ring (20 gauge)
- One 4mm silver-tone jump ring (22 gauge)
- One 12mm silver-tone lobster clasp
- Eleven 1½" (3.8 cm) silver-tone headpins

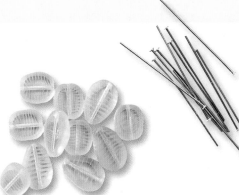

How to Make a Multi-Drop Necklace

1 Drape a piece of string around your neck at the place where you would like your necklace to hang. Measure the string to determine the length of chain you will need. Cut the chain to the measured length of the string using the cutters.

> **TIP** Since the necklace features a center drop with an odd number of beaded drops, you will want to have an odd number of loops in the length of chain that you cut. You may need to adjust the length of the chain to end up with an odd number of loops. Remember that the beaded drops add weight to the chain, so the necklace will hang a bit lower than a piece of string of the same length. Also, the clasp and loops at the back closure will add about 5⁄8″ (1.6 cm) to the finished length.

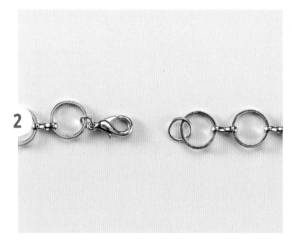

2 Open the 6.5mm *jump ring* by bending the ends away from each other perpendicular to the loop. Hook the jump ring through one end of the chain. Close the jump ring, aligning the ends so that there is no gap. Open the 4mm jump ring and hook it through the other end of the chain. Attach the lobster clasp to the jump ring and close the loop.

> **TIP** Loop and connector chain has a front and a back. Depending on whether you are right-handed or left-handed, put the clasp on the end of the necklace you prefer, making sure the chain is right-side up.

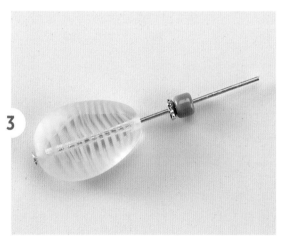

3 Slide a lime teardrop bead onto one headpin so the bead touches the flat part of the head-pin. Slide on one small silver-tone bead cap so that it touches and curves over the top of the teardrop bead. Slide on an opaque lime e-bead so that it touches the cap.

> **TIP** For a bead that is narrow or small at the top (like a teardrop or table-cut bead), select a cap that does not extend beyond the top edge of the bead. If the cap is too large, it may rub against your skin while you are wearing the necklace and cause irritation.

QUICK REFERENCE

Jump ring. Different manufacturers and suppliers have different ways of indicating jump ring size. In this book, the jump ring measurement indicated is the outside diameter of the ring, and the gauge indicated is the thickness of the wire of the jump ring.

4 Hold the stacked beads between your thumb and fingers, keeping all the beads stacked closely together touching the flat base of the headpin. Use chain-nose pliers to bend the wire at a right angle just above the top bead. Use either chain-nose or round-nose pliers to form a ⅛" (3 mm) loop by bending the headpin wire in the opposite direction of the first bend. Trim the loop so that it will be even once it is closed. Repeat steps 3 and 4 for all of the lime striped teardrops and the lime stripe rounded rectangles. Even though you are working with two different shapes of beads, all of the drops have the same caps and e-beads on top.

5 Hook a teardrop beaded drop on the center link of the chain, and then close the loop.

6 Hook a rounded rectangle beaded drop on the loops on either side of the center loop with the teardrop.

7 Continue to add drops, alternating the two shapes, until you have added them all to the chain.

Variations

Using repetition of elements, this bracelet uses drops with only one style
of bead on each drop. Instead of attaching the drops on a single necklace chain,
you start with a bracelet of three strands
of delicate chain with a distinctive loop
pattern. Each strand of chain has a different bead, but the same style of drop. By
layering the chains together, the bracelet
has a fringed look, with the repetition of
components creating the texture.

Like the necklace in the project, a loop
and connector chain makes up the base.
This time the two beads on the necklace
are different sizes, but have similar
shapes. Instead of attaching individual
drops to each chain loop, there are two
smaller and one larger drop on a loop,
and the drops repeat only every third
loop. By skipping loops and adding
drops all the way around the necklace
instead of just in the front, an undulating collar is the result. Patterns can be
designed with bead shape as well as
spacing choices.

Change the shapes and sizes (and even colors) of the beads on the drops, and you have a completely new look. Added variation comes from the change in the length of the drops, even if the basic elements on each drop are the same.

HEADPINS:
Beaded Cluster Bracelet

The two previous project designs used drops on headpins, and the sequence of beads on the headpins stayed the same. For a more complex design, the beads on each drop can be varied. This fun summery bracelet is made using all natural materials.

WHAT YOU'LL LEARN. . . . .

- How to make drops with an assortment of sizes and shapes of beads
- How to combine assorted drops together for a cluster look
- How to find a solution to using beads with different size holes
- How to create texture in a design

WHAT YOU'LL NEED. . . . .

TOOLS

- Chain-nose or round-nose pliers
- Wire cutters

MATERIALS

- 7¼" (18.4 cm) gold-tone medium oval loop and connector chain (¼" [6 mm] loops) (adjust for wrist size see page 31)

- 10 oz box Jewelry Essentials Naturals wood and shell bead mix
- Thirty-two 1½" (3.8 cm) gold-tone headpins
- One 6.5mm gold-tone jump ring (20 gauge)
- One 4mm gold-tone jump ring (22 gauge)
- One 12mm gold-tone lobster clasp

How to Make a Beaded Cluster Bracelet

1 For this bracelet you will need to make long *multi-bead drops* consisting of three or four beads stacked on the same headpin for each of the links on the chain. This sample chain has seventeen links, so you will need seventeen long drops. None of the drops on the bracelet are exactly the same, resulting in a very textured bracelet. For the first of the long drops slide a shell bead onto one headpin so that it touches the base on the headpin. Add a square taupe wood bead and a light colored textured wood bead. Hold the stacked beads between your thumb and fingers, keeping all the beads stacked closely together, touching the flat base of the headpin. Use chain-nose pliers to bend the wire at a 90-degree angle just above the top bead. Using either chain- or round-nose pliers, form a ⅛" (3 mm) loop by bending the headpin wire in the opposite direction of the first bend.

2 Repeat step 1 to create sixteen more long drops. Use a shell bead or other bead with a smaller hole at the base of each stack to prevent the beads with larger holes from slipping over the headpin. None of the drops on the bracelet are exactly the same.

3 Once all of the long drops have been created, use wire cutters to trim the loop on each drop so that it will be even once it is closed.

4 Open the 6.5mm jump ring by bending the ends away from each other perpendicular to the loop. Hook the jump ring through one end of the chain. Close the jump ring, aligning the ends so that there is no space between the ends. Open the 4mm jump ring and hook it through the other end of the chain. Attach the lobster clasp to the jump ring and close the loop.

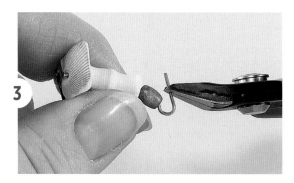

TIP Bead assortments will often include beads that have holes in a variety of sizes and directions. Beads with large holes will slip off over the head of the headpin. There are a number of different solutions to this problem. Bead caps or small seed beads can be used at the bottom of the stack to prevent slippage. For this bracelet, the shells, which have smaller holes, are used at the bottom of each drop in order to keep the rest of the stack on the headpin.

5

6

7

5 Lay the chain out on your work surface. Starting at the clasp end of the bracelet, attach one long drop to the right side of the first link of the chain. Attach the next long drop to the left side of the next link. Continue adding a long drop to each link, alternating sides of the bracelet. Use chain-nose pliers to close the loop on each drop to attach.

6 The sample bracelet has fifteen shorter drops, one drop for each link except for the two end links where the clasp and loop are attached. Make the short drops the same way that you made the long drops, but use one to three beads per drop. Clip all the headpins using the wire cutters.

7 Lay out the bracelet on your work surface. Starting at the clasp end, attach one short drop to the second link on the chain, on the opposite side from the long drop. Attach the next short drop to the next link, again on the opposite side of the long drop. Continue attaching short drops, alternating sides for each link. Use chain-nose pliers to close the loop on each drop to attach. Once all of your short drops are attached, your bracelet is complete.

QUICK REFERENCE

Multi-bead drops. When stacking different size and shape beads on a headpin to form a drop it is important that the drops are balanced. One way to maintain balance is to graduate the size of the beads from largest to smallest. Another is to not stack two beads of the same size directly on top of one another; if you want to use two beads of the same size, insert a spacer bead, a smaller bead, or a flat bead between them. Using different sizes and shapes of beads, plus making longer and shorter drops, gives variety and texture to the piece and makes it more interesting.

Variations

This cluster earring uses four different pearl colors, but all the same size bead. Placing one bead on each side (back, front, left side, right side) of a cable chain creates a box pattern cluster, with one of the colors of pearls on each side.

The drops on this necklace cluster pendant are hung from the back, front, left, and right side of the chain, but only on a few links. Lampwork beads are used in conjunction with fire-polished glass to give the pendant additional texture.

This cluster bracelet uses Czech fire-polished beads in the same color range, one bead per headpin. Larger beads are placed opposite smaller beads in the same manner as the long and short drops on the project piece.

EYE PINS:
Segmented Anklet

Eye pins present many options for connecting jewelry elements together. Applications include constructing your own beaded chains and lengthening drops for earrings. As you gain a better understanding of the function of eye pins, you will start to see the endless variety of ways you can assemble them to add complexity to your designs.

WHAT YOU'LL LEARN..

- How to create beaded segments using eye pins
- How to make a chain by linking beaded segments
- How to use slight color variations to create visual impact

- How to make an anklet adjustable
- How to add decorative drops as a finishing touch

WHAT YOU'LL NEED..

TOOLS

- Piece of string to measure ankle size
- Chain-nose or round-nose pliers
- Wire cutters
- Ruler

MATERIALS

- Fifteen to twenty-four 6 × 8mm pressed glass smooth oval beads: translucent purple, purple iris, rose (the number of oval beads will depend on the length of the anklet)

- Two 12mm pressed glass smooth star beads: purple AB, purple iris
- Fifteen to twenty-four ⅝" (1.6 cm) silver-tone eye pins (the number of eye pins needed depends on the size of your ankle)
- One 6.5mm silver-tone jump ring (20 gauge)
- One 4mm silver-tone jump ring (22 gauge)
- One 12mm silver-tone lobster clasp
- Two 1½" (3.8 cm) silver-tone headpins

How to Make a Segmented Anklet

1 Measure your ankle with a piece of string to determine its size. For this project, the clasp will add about ⅝" (1.6 cm) to the length of the anklet (refer to page 31). Start with a ⅝" (1.6 cm) eye pin and slide on one purple iris oval bead. Make a loop at the opposite end parallel to the first one (refer to page 26). Since these eye pins are quite short, you will not need to trim off the excess wire. Hook on another eye pin and close the loop.

TIP When making an anklet, first think about the type of footwear you will be wearing with it. You may need to add extra length if you wear socks under the anklet. A shorter length is better if you wear sandals with a heel strap. Also take into account walking and the movement of your foot. If the anklet is too short, it may break from constant strain.

2 Slide a translucent purple bead onto the second eye pin and make a loop at the opposite end. Add on an eye pin and close the loop.

3 Slide a rose bead onto the third eye pin and make a loop at the opposite end. Add on an eye pin and close the loop. Continue to add beads and repeat the colors of the beading pattern until you have enough beads for the desired anklet length.

4 Open the 6.5mm jump ring by bending the ends away from each other perpendicular to the loop. Hook the jump ring through one end of the chain. Close the jump ring, aligning the ends so that there is no space between the ends. Open the 4mm jump ring and hook it through the other end of the chain. Attach the lobster clasp to the jump ring and close the ring.

TIP When making a beaded chain using eye pins, make sure that the beads you use have large enough holes for the eye pin thickness you are using. Some stone beads, pearls, bugle beads, or seed beads may not fit on a standard thickness eye pin. If you use a thinner eye pin, make sure to keep the eye pin segments fairly short or they might bend while you are wearing the finished piece of jewelry.

5 On one headpin, slide on the purple iris star, with the top point facing up. Slide on a rose oval bead. Make a ⅛" (3 mm) loop at the top and trim the excess wire. Slide the purple AB star onto the other headpin, with the top point facing up. Make a ⅛" (3 mm) loop at the top and trim the excess wire.

6 *Attach both drops* to the 6.5mm jump ring at one end of the beaded chain.

QUICK REFERENCE

Attach both drops. If you finish the design by attaching a decorative drop to the end loop on the anklet (or bracelet), you will be able to adjust the length of the anklet by hooking the lobster clasp between the beads over the wire links not just through the jump ring. Just make sure that you are using a lobster clasp that is large enough to hook over the wire links but not so large that it will slide over the beads.

Variations

Try the same style of anklet using alternating shapes of stone beads. It is a good idea to select beads that will lie flat against the ankle.

Choose three colors of the same bead style and graduate the sizes, and then add a larger focal bead to make elegant, graduated, and segmented earrings. Use the colors in the focal bead to select the other bead colors in this design.

Make a graduated two-strand necklace with focal beads. The second strand will need to be shorter than the first to hang well when the necklace is worn. Change the pattern of the inside and the outside beaded chain strands to get the best balance between the beads and the two strands. Like the anklet project, the necklace is constructed from three colors of the same style of beads. This necklace uses four sizes of beads, plus there are three sizes of more complex cloisonné focal beads. An extra feature is the beaded extender, used for easy adjustment to the necklace length.

EYE PINS:
Double Triangle Earrings

Now that you have discovered the easiest way to use an eye pin, the fun really begins. You will start to experiment with some more creative construction using the same simple beaded eye pin elements. In this project, you will use multiple beads on one eye pin. You will also connect more than one eye pin together, and add a simple drop. The result is a simple, geometric, elegant earring style with many options for variations.

WHAT YOU'LL LEARN...

- How to add multiple beads to a single eye pin
- How to form new shapes with multiple eye pins by interlocking the end loops
- How to add a finishing drop on a headpin to function as both a decoration and a connecting element

WHAT YOU'LL NEED...

TOOLS

- Chain-nose or round-nose pliers
- Wire cutters

MATERIALS

- Thirty-two 4mm Czech fire-polished faceted beads: black

- Ten 1″ (2.5 cm) gold-tone eye pins
- Two 4mm gold-tone jump rings (22 gauge)
- Two gold-tone lever-back wires
- Two ⅝″ (1.6 cm) gold-tone headpins

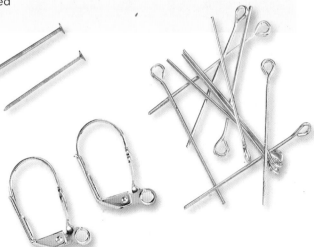

How to Make Double Triangle Earrings

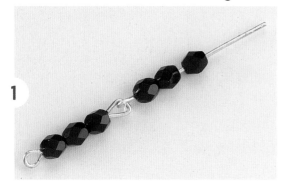

1 Slide three 4mm black beads onto one eye pin. Using chain-nose pliers, bend the end of the wire at a right angle at the top of the last bead, making sure to not crack the bead. Bend the wire in the opposite direction to form a ⅛" (3 mm) loop. Make sure the loop is parallel to the loop on the opposite end of the eye pin. Trim off excess wire. Hook the open loop through the closed loop of another eye pin. Close the loop. Add three black 4mm beads to the second eye pin.

2 Finish the loop on the second eye pin and attach another eye pin. The loop should be parallel to the loop on the opposite end of the eye pin. Add three beads to the third eye pin. Bend, cut, and close the loop on the third eye pin.

3 Open one of the 4mm jump rings by bending the ends away from each other perpendicular to the direction of the ring. Hook one end of the short beaded eye pin chain that you have made onto the jump ring. Slide the other end of the linked chain onto the jump ring, making sure not to twist the links. The three beaded eye pins will form a neat triangle.

4 Slide the open jump ring on the beaded eye pin triangle through the hanging loop on one of the lever-back wires. Close the jump ring so the ends are once again flush, and the beaded triangle dangles freely from the hook.

TIP If you decide to use longer eye pins for a larger design, make sure not to stack too many beads on the eye pins. If the individual sections become too long, the eye pins are prone to bending, which will distort your triangles.

5 Open the loop on one nonbeaded eye pin by bending the cut end of the loop perpendicular to the direction of the loop. Hook the loop through the bottom side of the loop of the beaded eye pin that forms the crossbar of the triangle. Close the loop.

6 Add three black beads and form the loop on the other end of the eye pin, making it parallel to the loop on the opposite end of the eye pin.

7 Repeat step 5, adding an eye pin to the bottom at the other end of the triangle. Add three black beads, and close the loop as you did on the other side.

8 Slide a black bead onto a ⅝" (1.6 cm) headpin. Bend the wire on top of the bead at a right angle. Bending the wire back in the opposite direction, form a ⅛" (3 mm) loop. Trim the excess wire.

9 Hook the open loop of the drop through the two bottom loops of the eye pins attached to the bottom of the triangle. Close the loop on the drop: this will form a second inverted triangle. Repeat the steps to make a second double triangle earring.

6

7

8

9

5

Variations

To add a little texture to your double triangle earring design, vary the size of the beads on each eye pin.

Using smaller beads, you can create a fun, elongated earring by linking two double triangles together. Also experiment with mixing up the colors of the beads.

Create a whole new look by mixing the style, size, and color of the beads. As you add more double triangle elements and combine them with single beaded eye pin connectors, you can make an attractive chain perfect for a bracelet or a necklace.

EYE PINS:
Textured Segmented Necklace

This project combines a simple beaded chain with eye pins with a more complex link construction. Seed beads on double eye pin sections add a double stranded look, as well as give a bit more weight and detail to the finished piece. A tassel made of both beaded headpins and eye pins gives this easy-to-construct necklace a far more elaborate look.

WHAT YOU'LL LEARN . . . .

- How to vary your loop size so you can link multiple eye pins together
- How to vary the bead shapes and sizes to create interest
- How to make a focal point tassel
- How to integrate beads with unpredictable hole sizes
- How to create a multiple strand look with simple segments

WHAT YOU'LL NEED . . . .

TOOLS

- Chain-nose pliers
- Round-nose pliers
- Wire cutters

MATERIALS

- Size 10/0 seed beads on string: translucent red
- Eleven 9 × 16mm triangular pressed glass beads: translucent red with AB finish

- Twenty-one 4mm Czech druk beads: red
- Eight 9 × 5mm thick triangular furnace beads: red stripe
- Twenty-seven 1½" (3.8 cm) gold-tone eye pins
- Three 1" (2.5 cm) eye pins
- Three 1½" (3.8 cm) gold-tone headpins
- One 6.5mm gold-tone jump ring (20 gauge)
- One 4mm gold-tone jump ring (22 gauge)
- One gold-tone 12mm lobster clasp

How to Make a Textured Segmented Necklace

TIP When you select the seed beads and eye pins for this project, choose seed beads with holes that are large enough to slide onto the pins. You do not want to use eye pins that are too thin, or the segments of your necklace will bend with wearing.

1 Pull a small grouping of seed beads off of the string between your thumb and finger and slide them onto a 1½" (3.8 cm) eye pin. Repeat this until the beads fill the pin up to ¼" (6 mm) from the end. With chain-nose pliers, bend the wire at the top of the beads at a right angle. Make a tight loop with the remaining wire, and close the loop. The loop should be parallel to the loop on the opposite end of the eye pin. Repeat this step until you have twelve eye pins covered with seed beads.

TIP If you purchase seed beads that are strung rather than loose, it will make the process of putting them on the eye pins faster and easier.

2 Open the 6.5mm jump ring perpendicular to the direction of the loop. Hook the ring through one end of two of the seed bead eye pins. Close the ring. Set this piece aside. Open the 4mm jump ring, attach the clasp, and then attach two of the seed bead eye pins. Close the ring.

3 Open the loop on a 1½" (3.8 cm) eye pin. Hook on the loop of a second 1½" (3.8 cm) eye pin and close the loop. Slide a pressed glass triangular bead onto one of the two eye pins with the wide base toward the loops.

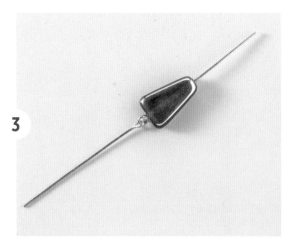

4 Bend the wire at the pointed end of the triangle at a right angle. With round-nose pliers, make a ¼" (6 mm) loop and trim excess wire. Slide the loose ends of the two seed bead eye pins that are connected by a jump ring onto the loop. Close the large loop, attaching the seed bead eye pins.

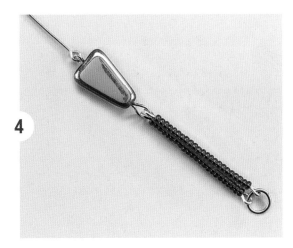

5 Place a 4mm druk bead, a furnace bead, and another druk bead onto the empty 1½" (3.8 cm) eye pin. Make a ⅛" (3 mm) loop and trim the excess wire. Hook on another 1½" (3.8 cm) eye pin, and close the loop.

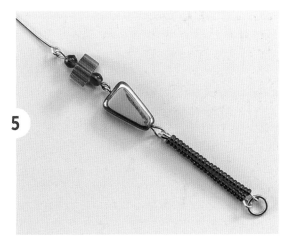

6 Slide a pressed triangle bead onto the empty eye pin, with the wide base facing toward the furnace bead. Make a ¼" (6 mm) loop, and trim the excess wire. Slide two seed bead eye pins onto the open loop and close it.

(continued)

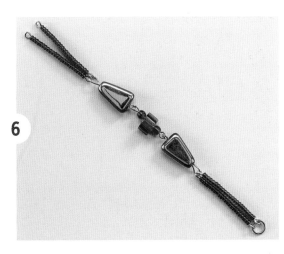

7 Repeat steps 3 to 6 with the third set of seed bead eye pins being the last things you attach. Starting with the seed bead eye pins attached to the clasp, make the second side of the necklace to look just like the first.

8 Open the loop on one 1½" (3.8 cm) eye pin, and hook on two other 1½" (3.8 cm) eye pins. Close the loop. On the first eye pin, add a druk bead, a furnace bead, and another druk bead. Next to the second druk bead, form a ¼" (6 mm) loop.

9 Slide one druk bead onto each of the other two empty 1½" (3.8 cm) eye pins and make a ¼" (6 mm) loop on each. Trim the excess wire on all three eye pins.

10 Onto a 1½" (3.8 cm) headpin slide a druk bead, a furnace bead, another druk bead, and a pressed glass triangle with the pointed end toward the top of the headpin. Repeat this step to make two more drops.

8

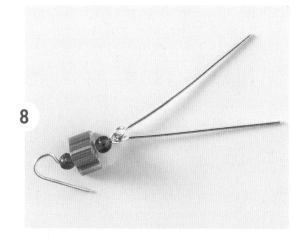

9

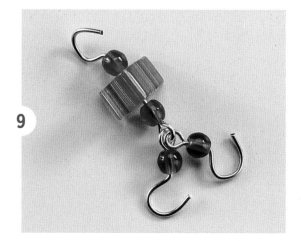

10

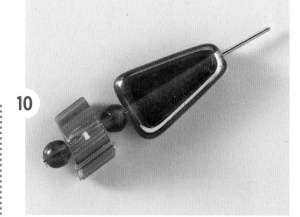

QUICK REFERENCE

Attach drops together. In order to keep the balance between the double stranded look of the necklace and the focal drop, constructing a tassel of multiple drops will add weight to the centerpiece.

11 Form a ⅛" (3 mm) loop on the first beaded drop, trim excess wire, attach a 1" (2.5 cm) eye pin, and close the loop. Slide a druk bead onto the eye pin, make a ⅛" (3 mm) loop, and trim the excess wire. Close the loop. Repeat this step to lengthen the other two drops.

12 **Attach drops together** by hooking all three drops on the ¼" (6 mm) loop at the bottom of the furnace bead segment and closing the loop.

13 Assemble the necklace. Attach one side of the necklace by hooking the two seed bead segments to the ¼" (6 mm) loop on the small druk bead segment next to the center drop. Close the loop. Repeat this step for the other side of the necklace.

11

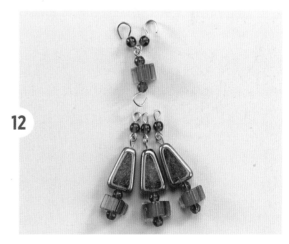

12

13

Variations

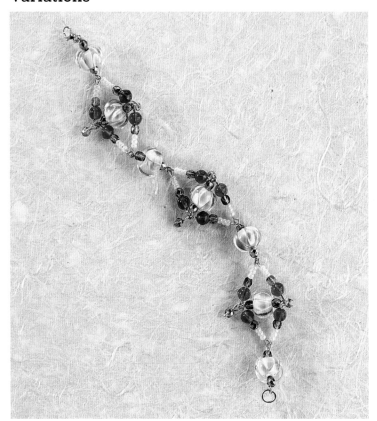

This bracelet is similar to the one on page 63. The smaller beaded segments combine three sizes and styles of beads in an asymmetrical pattern. The undulating transition from one focal lampwork bead to the next creates the appearance of movement. Added side drops enhance this effect.

When you feel confident with making eye pin segments and varying loop sizes, try more complex assembly. Notice how the loops on the eye pins aid in the soft drape of the earrings and add a decorative element. The color fade in the crystals enhances the overall design.

For this eyeglass chain, the double eye pin segments with seed beads were replaced with long twisted bugle bead segments for a more linear, elegant look. The larger beads were replaced with delicate glass pearls alternated with spacer beads and e-beads. Using all small beads produces a chainlike look, yet maintains the interest of a double strand.

JUMP RINGS:
Interlocking Jump Ring Earrings

Jump rings have often been thought of as strictly functional findings, mostly used to connect one jewelry element to another. However, jump rings, combined in multiples, can become more than just functional elements. In addition to learning how to make a decorative double-link chain from jump rings, you will select a bead to best coordinate with the chain. Jump ring chain made with round loops has a clean look, with the emphasis on the circular elements. For the earring project, you will use round disk beads to emphasize the round elements of the rings.

WHAT YOU'LL LEARN. . . . .

- How to open and close jump rings
- How to attach jump rings together to make a simple linked chain
- How to add a beaded drop to a chain element for extra interest
- How to choose a bead to complement the jump ring chain

WHAT YOU'LL NEED. . . . .

TOOLS

- Chain-nose pliers (two pairs)
- Round-nose pliers
- Wire cutters
- Jump ring tool (optional)

MATERIALS

- Two 20mm disk lampwork beads: aventurine with millefiore
- Twenty-four 6.5mm silver-tone jump rings (20 gauge)
- Two silver-tone French ear wires
- Two 1½" (3.8 cm) silver-tone headpins

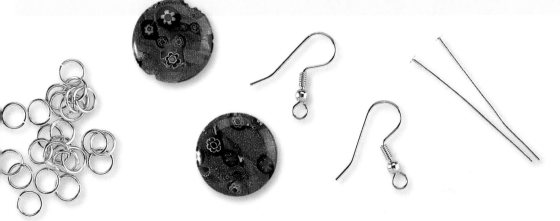

How to Make Interlocking Jump Ring Earrings

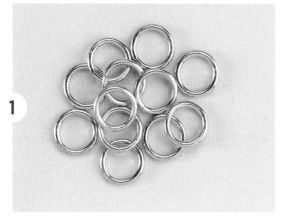

1 If your **jump rings** come out of the package already closed, skip this step and set aside twelve of the closed rings. If they come out of the package slightly split open (the cut ends do not meet), close twelve rings by bending the cut ends toward each other using chain-nose pliers and your finger, two pairs of chain-nose pliers, or a jump ring tool. Bend the ends perpendicular to the direction of the ring. Make sure cut ends are flush with each other and completely aligned.

TIP When working with multiple jump rings in a project, you may wish to purchase a jump ring tool, which will aid you in opening and closing jump rings quickly and easily.

2 If your jump rings come out of the package closed, open twelve rings so that the gap is wide enough to slide two other jump rings through.

3 Slide four closed jump rings onto one open ring. Close the ring.

4 Loop another open jump ring over the same four closed jump rings and close it. Separate the four loops so that you have a short chain of three links of two loops each.

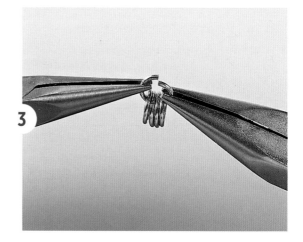

5 Attach an open jump ring to one two-loop end of the chain and add two closed rings. Close the ring.

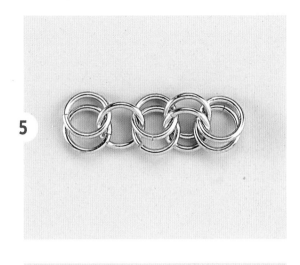

6 Add a second open jump ring next to the first one, connecting the two sets of double rings. Again, be sure not to accidentally hook the second jump ring through the first, or your chain will not hang straight. You should now have five double-ring links in your chain.

7 Attach another open jump ring to one end of the five-link chain. Close the ring. Add a second jump ring next to the first and close it, completing the last link.

(continued)

QUICK REFERENCE

Jump rings. For this project, as with the subsequent jump ring projects in this chapter, the jump ring measurement indicated is the outside diameter of the ring, and the gauge indicated is the thickness of the wire of the jump ring. As you work more frequently with jump rings in your designs, you may want to test several different sizes and gauges to find the ones that work best for you. If the gauge is too high (meaning it is made with a thin wire), the jump ring may be too soft and delicate to hold components together. If the gauge is too low, and the jump ring is too thick, you may have trouble manipulating the ring to close it cleanly with no gap.

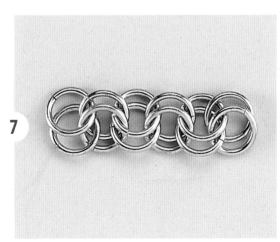

8 Open the loop on the earring hook the same way you opened the jump rings: bend the cut end away from the rest of the hook perpendicular to the direction of the loop. Hook the open earring loop through one end of the six-link chain.

9 Slide a round disk bead onto a headpin so that it touches the end. Bend the wire above the bead at a 90-degree angle, making sure not to chip the bead. Bend the wire in the opposite direction to make a ⅛" (3 mm) loop. Trim excess wire.

10 Hook the bead drop onto the bottom end of the jump ring chain and close the loop. Use the remaining jump rings and repeat the steps to make the second earring.

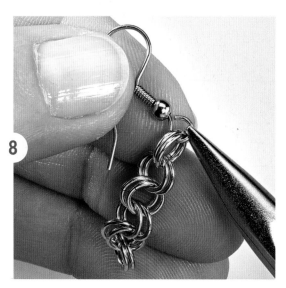

Variations

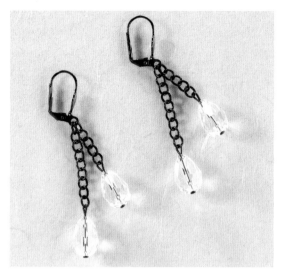

You can also create a simple chain by attaching single jump rings of the same size and color. For this pair of earrings, the gunmetal jump rings are oval. To add some interest to the earrings, two chains of different lengths were made for each earring, and then hooked directly on the earring hook. In this case, the longer chain hangs in the back, and the shorter one in the front, with a crystal drop added to each chain.

With the rings scaled down in this double-loop chain, more emphasis is placed on the square and rectangular stone components that contrast with the circular pattern in the chain.

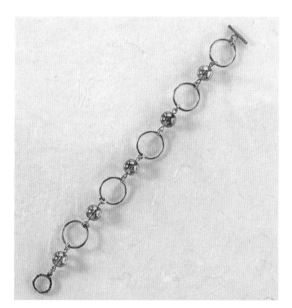

Single and double jump ring connections with dramatic size differences in the rings make an eye-catching design. The addition of medium sized smooth round beads and a toggle clasp emphasize the circular elements.

JUMP RINGS:
Jump Ring and Bead Necklace

Now that you have mastered the technique of creating your own chain, explore the infinite possibilities of color, loop, and bead variations. This time you will use a combination of gold- and silver-tone rings of different sizes to create the chain. In addition, you will make a single- and double-ring pattern, adding small beads to the larger single loops for an entirely different look. With jump rings you can create a customized chain with a smooth transition to a center drop without a break in the pattern.

WHAT YOU'LL LEARN. . . . .

- How to make a single- and double-ring pattern chain

- How to add beads to connecting rings for texture

- How to mix colors of jump rings

- How to combine different sizes of rings as a decorative element

- How to join two jump ring chain sections for a smooth transition to a center drop

- How to use a toggle clasp as a design element

WHAT YOU'LL NEED. . . . .

TOOLS

- Chain-nose pliers (two pairs)

- Round-nose pliers

- Wire cutters

- Jump ring tool (optional)

MATERIALS

- 113 glass e-beads (6/0): periwinkle opal

- One 20 × 25mm faceted blue stone bead with top to bottom hole

- One hundred sixteen 5mm silver-tone jump rings (20 gauge)

- Fifty-six 6.5mm gold-tone jump rings (20 gauge)

- One 2" (5.1 cm) silver-tone headpin

- One 13mm loop and 17mm bar silver-tone decorative toggle clasp

How to Make a Jump Ring and Bead Necklace

1 **Close jump rings.** Close four 5mm silver-tone jump rings.

2 Open one 6.5mm gold-tone jump ring so that the gap is wide enough to slide on a 6/0 e-bead. Slide on one blue e-bead, and then two of the closed silver rings. Slide on a second blue e-bead, and then the other two silver rings.

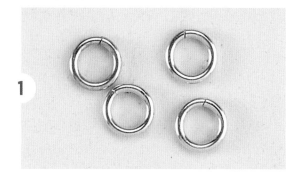

TIP When adding beads to a jump ring project, make certain that each bead has a large enough hole to fit over the jump rings but is small enough in diameter that you can close the jump ring cleanly around it and the additional rings you will add to make the chain.

3 Close two more 5mm silver-tone jump rings. As you did in step 2, open one gold-tone 6.5mm jump ring so that the gap is wide enough to slide a 6/0 e-bead on. Slide on one blue e-bead, and then two of the closed silver jump rings on one end of the chain you have started. Slide on a second blue e-bead, and then the two closed silver rings. Close the gold jump ring. Continue this pattern to make the chain for the center drop until you have five pairs of silver jump rings and four beaded gold jump rings.

4 Slide the stone bead onto a 2" (5.1 cm) headpin. Add a blue e-bead. Bend the wire at a right angle at the top of the beads, form a ⅛" (3 mm) loop, and trim the excess wire.

TIP Some stone beads have very small holes, so you may wish to use a bead reamer to widen the hole, or select a slightly thinner headpin. If the headpin is too thin, the loop on the drop may not stay closed and keep the drop in place.

5 Hook the loop on the blue stone drop onto one end of the chain. Close the loop.

6 Close four 5mm silver-tone jump rings. Open a gold jump ring and hook it through the top two silver rings on the center drop chain. Add a blue e-bead, add all four of the silver rings, and then add another blue e-bead. Carefully close the gold jump ring.

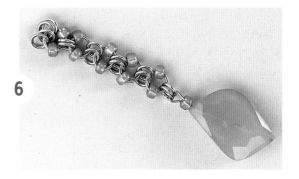

7 Close two 5mm silver-tone jump rings. Open a 6.5mm gold-tone jump ring and hook it through two of the four silver rings on the top of the center drop chain. Add a blue e-bead, add the two silver-tone rings, and then add another blue e-bead. Carefully close the gold jump ring. Repeat this step on the other two silver loops at the top of the center drop chain. This will start both chains that form the necklace. Continue to add silver rings and beaded gold rings until the necklace reaches the desired length.

TIP Make sure you have extra jump rings and beads, in case you decide to lengthen the necklace.

8 When you reach the last gold-tone ring with blue beads, use the last two silver-tone rings to attach each end of the toggle clasp to the necklace.

TIP If your toggle clasp does not have large enough holes for two jump rings, just use one on each end to attach the bar and loop.

QUICK REFERENCE

Close jump rings. If you know the approximate length of your necklace, you may wish to close all of the smaller silver jump rings before starting assembly, rather than closing them as you go, making assembly much faster.

Variations

This bracelet uses one tone and size of jump ring. Similar to the necklace, it starts with a single-and double-ring chain. Make two chains of equal length, where the single connector ring has a bead on only one side. Line up the chains next to each other with the beaded edges to the outside, and use a jump ring with one bead to connect the two chains together through a set of double rings from each chain. Make sure you attach corresponding double rings, or the bracelet will be uneven once both sides are linked together.

The base structure of these earrings is a series of graduated lengths of the single- and double-ring chain in gunmetal jump rings that are all the same size, attached to a simple round hoop component. E-beads are added to the double-ring components on the front and the back of the earrings using smaller silver- tone jump rings. Since the hoop has a center loop, drops are added to finish the design.

For some added color, use two different colors of e-beads and jump rings. The construction on this necklace is similar to the project, with crystal and polymer clay beads on eye pins periodically replacing the double-loop connectors. Adding larger bead elements completely changes the texture and scale of the necklace.

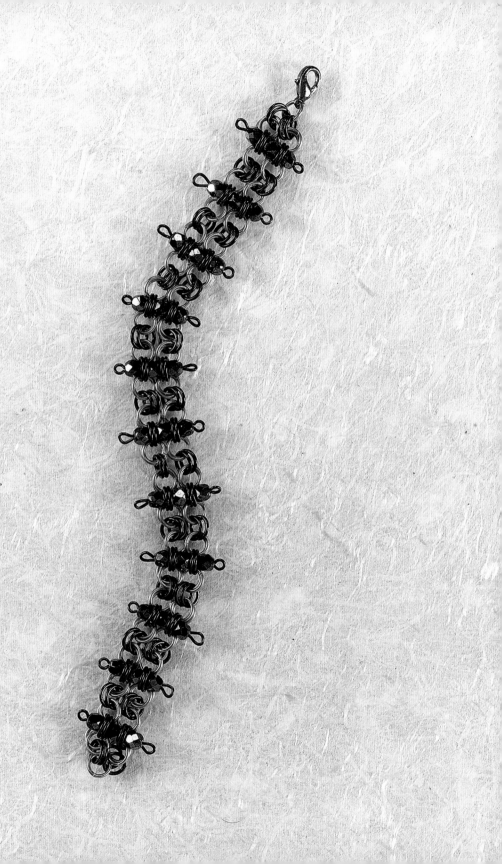

JUMP RINGS:
Jump Ring Lace Bracelet

In addition to combining jump rings of different colors and sizes, here is another way to add beads for an even more dimensional look. For this project, the eye pins will act as connectors for two jump ring chains, but the end loops will be used as decorative elements to create a lacy effect. The overall result is an elegant, flowing cuff bracelet with delicate details.

WHAT YOU'LL LEARN. . . . .

- How to connect two jump ring chains
- How to use eye pins as both decorative and functional elements
- How to add larger beaded elements to jump ring styles

WHAT YOU'LL NEED. . . . .

TOOLS

- Chain-nose pliers (2 pairs)
- Round-nose pliers
- Wire cutters
- Jump ring tool (optional)

MATERIALS

- Thirty-three 4mm Czech fire-polished beads: hematite
- Ninety 5mm copper-tone jump rings (20 gauge)
- Ninety-two 5mm gunmetal jump rings (20 gauge)
- One 11mm gunmetal lobster claw clasp
- Eleven ⅞" (2.2 cm) gunmetal eye pins

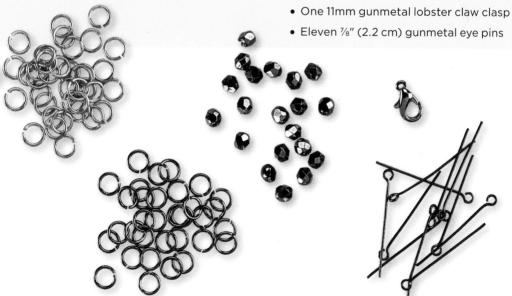

How to Make a Jump Ring Lace Bracelet

1 Close four of the 5mm copper jump rings. Hook all four jump rings onto a gunmetal ring and close it.

TIP When working with multiple jump rings in a project, you may wish to purchase a jump ring tool, which will aid you in opening and closing jump rings quickly and easily. You can also use a second pair of chain-nose pliers to help close the rings.

2 Hook a second gunmetal ring next to the first one and close it.

3 Add a gunmetal ring to one end of the started chain and close it. Add a second gunmetal ring next to the first one and close it.

4 Close all of the copper rings except for two. Add copper and gunmetal rings to the first chain you started as you did before. End the first chain with two gunmetal rings. Repeat the process to make a second chain the same length. The bracelet pictured has twenty-two sets of copper rings on each chain, and twenty-three sets of gunmetal rings. Once you have made the two chains, hook a copper ring through the gunmetal rings on one end of each chain and close it. On the other end of both chains hook a copper ring, add the clasp, and close the ring.

TIP Make sure to have extra rings to extend the length of the bracelet if necessary. The project pictured is 7" (17.8 cm) long. Measure your wrist before starting and check your chain lengths before linking them together. The clasp and loops will add ⅝" (1.6 cm) to the chain length. For a shorter length, shorten the chains.

5 Slide a hematite bead onto one of the ⅞" (2.2 cm) gunmetal eye pins. Starting at the clasp end of the bracelet, skip the first set of gunmetal rings and slide the eye pin through the second set of gunmetal rings on one of the two chains. Add a bead, and slide the eye pin through the corresponding gunmetal rings on the second chain. Add a third bead to the eye pin, and then bend the wire at the end of the bead at a right angle. Form a loop the same size as the one on the opposite end of the eye pin, facing in the same direction, trim the excess wire, and close the loop. Skip the next set of gunmetal rings and add a beaded eye pin to the fourth set of gunmetal rings.

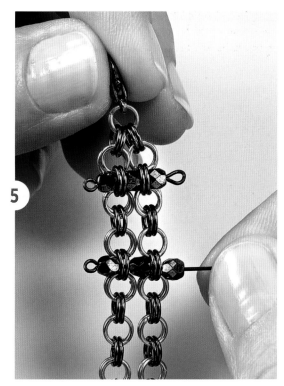

6 Repeat step 5 to connect the two chains at every other set of gunmetal rings for the entire length of the bracelet. Depending on the lengths of the chains you are using, you may have one or two sets of gunmetal rings with no beaded eye pin at the other end of the bracelet.

Variations

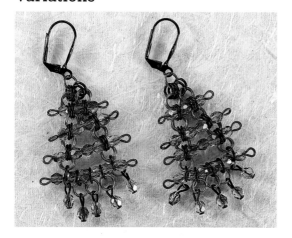

Like the bracelet project, the earrings use a double-double ring chain in a mix of the copper and gunmetal rings of the same size. This time, the eye pin connectors still use the same size 4mm Czech fire-polished glass beads, but the lengths of the eye pins graduate from short to long with added beads creating a triangular element for earring drops. The bottom eye pin has jump rings between the beads so that another set of rings and small beaded drops can be added to finish the bottom edge of the design.

For this necklace, start with a double-double ring chain, using larger loops than the bracelet and earrings in gold and silver tone. Find the center of the necklace chain and then make additional chains to hang equidistant from the center of the necklace chain. A graduated beaded drop connects the bottom of the two added chains. Add three beaded eye pins of graduated lengths to form an inverted triangle drop. The varied bead sizes give additional interest to the centerpiece.

This lace bracelet combines the beaded loop technique of the necklace project (page 79) with the decorative eye pin connector technique of this bracelet project. The seed beads were scaled down in order to add more beads to each ring, and the connector beads are a combination of 4mm Czech fire-polished and tube beads, with eye pins at every link instead of every other link. The bracelet can be worn with the eye pins facing the outside or the inside, for two completely different looks.

BEADING CABLE:
Teardrop Leaf Earrings

Beading cable, also called beading wire, is one of many options for stringing beads. This fine, strong cable is made of multiple strands of stainless steel or other metal with a nylon coating. The more strands within the cable, the more flexible it is. Beading cable holds its shape without kinking so looped design elements will keep their original form. Instead of knots, crimp tubes are used to finish the ends of beading cable.

WHAT YOU'LL LEARN..

- How to use crimp beads
- How to make loop elements with beading cable
- How to add beads with tip drilled holes
- How to make a hanging loop on a beading cable loop

WHAT YOU'LL NEED..

TOOLS

- Chain-nose pliers
- Crimp pliers
- Wire cutters
- Ruler

MATERIALS

- 14" (35.6 cm) beading cable: .015", 49 strands
- About 100 or 5½" (14 cm) of strung size 11/0 seed beads: topaz with AB finish
- Six 8 × 12mm leaf shaped beads with a tip drilled hole: olive with ghost (matte AB) finish on one side
- Four 2mm gold-tone crimp tubes
- Two gold-tone lever-back wires

How to Make Teardrop Leaf Earrings

1 Cut the 14" (35.6 cm) piece of beading cable
in half. Starting with one half, use chain-nose
pliers to flatten a **crimp tube** on to the very end of
the cable. Start to string the seed beads onto the
other end until you have 1¼" (3.2 cm) of seed beads
on the cable.

> **TIP** Select seed beads that are pre-strung on thread,
> it will make sliding the seed beads onto the cable
> go quickly.

2 String the first leaf onto the cable with the
matte AB side facing toward you.

3 Add two seed beads. Slide the second leaf on
with the olive side facing toward you.

4 Add two seed beads. Slide the third leaf
onto the cable with the matte AB side facing
toward you. Add 1¼" (3.2 cm) of seed beads.

QUICK REFERENCE

Crimp tube. By placing a crimp on one end, stringing
the beads on the entire earring design will be easy,
and the beads will not fall off in the process.

**Align the domed side of the groove with the front of the
earring.** By carefully aligning the direction of the crimp
on the tube, you can control the direction that the loop at
the top faces. This helps your teardrop face forward when
it is attached to the ear wire.

5 Slide all of the beads toward the center of the cable. Clip off the crimp bead from the end. Slide a new crimp bead over both ends of the cable, and pull it all the way down until it touches the beads on both sides.

6 Form a loop with both cables through the hole in the lever-back wire, and run the ends of the cable back through the crimp tube. Place the crimp tube into the inner groove of the crimp pliers. Align the domed side of the groove with the front of the earring, and the indented side with the back of the earring. Press the crimp tube in place. Place the crimp sideways in the outer groove of the crimp pliers and compress the crimp tube. Trim off the excess cable. Repeat all steps to make the second earring.

TIP Do not make the cable loop at the top of the earring too small or the teardrop hoop will not dangle freely, and do not make it so large that it looks odd. Pull both cables in the loop to the same length.

5

6

Variations

Try the same earring with a double loop of cable. You can make the earring even more fun by adding a variety of color-coordinated beads. With the double loop, you will only be able to get two of the strands to pass through the small crimp tube a second time. The crimp tube will hold all strands in place. It also looks better to only have two strands pass through the earring loop instead of four.

Create beaded hoops by running the cable strands through the crimp tube in opposite directions, then form the hanging loop with only one strand by bending it in the opposite direction over the top of the crimp tube, and inserting it back through the tube. Once a loop is formed, crimp the bead flat with chain-nose pliers instead of crimp pliers, parallel to the surface of the loop, and trim off the excess cable. This version does not have drops; instead the texture is created by graduating the beads, varying the shapes, and adding rondelles for sparkle.

This necklace can be strung from the center to help balance the design. As you did with the teardrop hoops, cut the full length of cable you will need and flat crimp a bead on one end. Make all of the drops in advance, and then start by forming the center loop and working to one end. The loops are made like the ones in the round hoop earrings (opposite), where the cable is passed through the crimp tube at the top of the loop in opposite direction, and then crimped flat. Once you have worked out the spacing of the loops and half the length of the necklace, finish the first end with a clasp, remove the crimp on the opposite end, and string the second half of the necklace.

BEADING CABLE:
Long Beaded Necklace

For this project you will string a simple 34" to 35" (86.5 to 89 cm) necklace on beading cable. Groups of smaller beads separate polymer clay focal beads and allow them to stand out. At this length, the necklace can be worn long or doubled for versatility. It is important to consider the weight of the beads on a longer necklace. Larger, heavier beads may make a necklace uncomfortable and would require a thicker beading cable.

WHAT YOU'LL LEARN . . . .

- How to make a basic beaded necklace
- How to use focal beads in a longer necklace

WHAT YOU'LL NEED . . . .

TOOLS

- Crimp pliers
- Chain-nose pliers
- Wire cutters
- Ruler

MATERIALS

- 38" (96.5 cm) beading cable: .015", 49 strands
- Five 13mm square polymer clay beads or other focal beads

- 320 size 8/0 seed beads: multi-amethyst ghost
- Sixteen 6 × 6mm faceted bicone beads: matte amethyst
- Six Czech fire-polished 8mm faceted beads: light amethyst
- Four 11mm coin shaped shell beads: lavender
- One 4mm silver-tone jump ring (22 gauge)
- One 6.5mm silver-tone jump ring (20 gauge)
- One 12mm silver-tone lobster clasp
- Two 2mm silver-tone crimp tubes

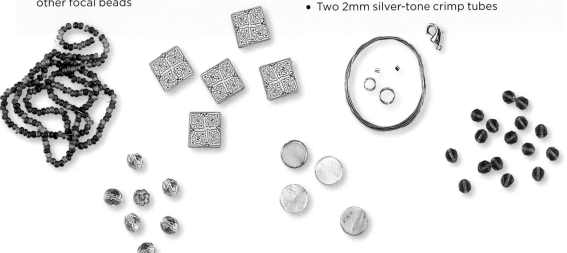

How to Make a Long Beaded Necklace

1 *Determine length.* Cut a piece of beading cable that is about 4" (10.2 cm) longer than the desired necklace length. In this project, a 38" (96.5 cm) piece of beading cable was used. Slide one of the focal beads onto the center of the beading cable.

TIP By starting to bead in the center of the necklace you can ensure that the pattern is symmetrical. You can also stop the pattern when you reach the predetermined necklace length. Knot one end of the cable or place a crimp at the end to prevent beads from sliding off. That way you can bead one side of the necklace first, finish the end, and then go back and bead the other side. If you want to bead both sides at once, it helps to hold both ends of the beading cable in one hand.

2 Add ten seed beads on each side of the focal bead. Then add a bicone bead and ten more seed beads to both sides.

TIP When stringing necklaces with sections of seed beads it is easier to buy the seed beads that are already on a thread rather than loose beads. This way they can be strung directly from the string onto the beading cable.

3 Add a Czech fire-polished bead to both sides of the necklace, followed by ten seed beads, one bicone bead, and then ten more seed beads.

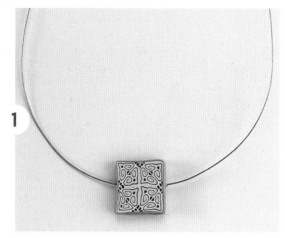

4 Add a shell bead to each side of the necklace followed by ten seed beads, one bicone bead, and ten more seed beads. Add a focal bead to each side of the necklace to complete the pattern. Repeat the pattern for the required length.

5 Attach the 4mm jump ring onto the loop of the clasp. Slide a crimp tube onto one end of the beading cable, making sure that the other end is secure so you won't lose any beads. Pull the cable end through the 4mm jump ring. Bring the cable back through the crimp bead and pull in excess cable, forming a ³⁄₃₂" (2.4 mm) loop between the crimp bead and the jump ring. Use crimp pliers to crimp the tube in place and trim off excess cable with wire cutters.

6 Slide a crimp tube onto the other end of the necklace. Pull the cable through the 6.5mm jump ring. Bring the cable back through the crimp bead and pull in excess cable, forming a ³⁄₃₂" (2.4 mm) loop between the crimp bead and the jump ring. Use crimp pliers to crimp the tube in place and trim off excess cable with wire cutters.

4

5

6

QUICK REFERENCE

Determine length. In order to make a necklace that you can wear both long or short, you may want to start by determining the most comfortable length for you in a short necklace and then double that length for the long necklace. For most people a comfortable short length is between 16" and 19" (40.6 and 48.3 cm). Make sure to add a few inches to your measurement so you have enough cable to crimp at the ends.

Variations

Change the look of the longer necklace by using a larger quantity of longer focal beads with fewer seed beads between them.

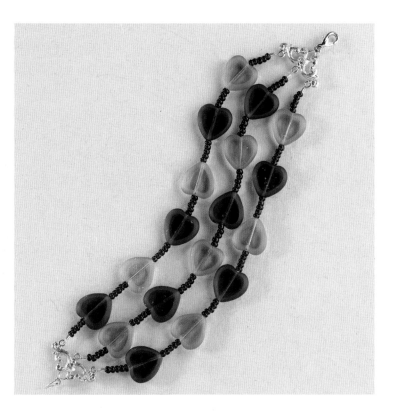

This three-strand bracelet uses the same focal bead in two different colors with seed beads between them.

The drops of these triple drop earrings are made by running beading cable through a single seed bead and then putting both ends of the cable through the bottom focal bead the seed beads, and a crimping tube. After forming the hanging loop, all four strands are crimped together.

BEADING CABLE:
Woven Bracelet with Pearls

Once you are familiar with beading cable, you can start to play with more complex variations. This bracelet is made by weaving two cable strands through the beads to create the look of a multi-strand bracelet. As you gain experience, you will discover how to change the color and the bead sizes to make a wide variety of textured accessories.

WHAT YOU'LL LEARN..

- How to use a box-and-tongue clasp for multiple strands of beading
- How to work with two strands of beading cable to create a woven, multi-strand look
- How seed beads used as spacers can be a key design element

WHAT YOU'LL NEED..

TOOLS

- Chain-nose or round-nose pliers
- Wire cutters
- Crimp pliers
- String to measure wrist

MATERIALS

- 40" to 44" (101.6 to 111.8 cm) beading cable: .015", 49 strand

- Twenty to twenty-three 8mm Czech fire-polished faceted beads: garnet
- Seventy-six to eighty-eight size 11/0 seed beads: matte gold
- Thirty-eight to forty-eight 6 × 4mm button freshwater pearls: bronze
- Four 2mm gold-tone crimp tubes
- One $7/16$" × $9/16$" (1.1 × 1.4 cm) gold-tone two-strand box-and-tongue clasp

How to Make a Woven Bracelet with Pearls

1 *Measure your wrist* with a piece of string to determine the size of your wrist. For this project, the clasp will add about ⅝" (1.6 cm) to the length of the bracelet. Once you have decided on a finished length, cut two pieces of beading cable that are each two-and-one-half times the length of the calculated beaded portion of the bracelet. Slide a crimp bead on the end of one piece of the beading cable. Thread the end of the cable through one loop on the box end of the clasp. Slide the cable back through the crimp bead and pull the short end of the cable to form a small ³⁄₃₂" (2.4 mm) loop between the crimp bead and the loop on the clasp. Use crimp pliers to crimp the bead in place. Trim off the excess cable.

2 Repeat this step to crimp the second piece of cable onto the second loop on the box portion of the clasp.

3 Slide a fire-polished bead onto one of the two cable strands. Pull the other cable strand through the bead in the opposite direction. Pull the ends of both cables until the bead slides up next to the clasp.

> ## QUICK REFERENCE
>
> *Measure your wrist.* When measuring your wrist size to determine bracelet length, remember to include the length of the type of clasp you are using. Make the bracelet long enough so that you can close the clasp yourself, but not so long that it will slide over your hand while the clasp is shut. Generally, a comfortable bracelet measurement is 1" (2.5 cm) longer than your wrist measurement. A bit more may be added to accommodate larger beads.

1

2

3

4 Onto one strand, string a gold seed bead, a pearl, and another seed bead. Do the same on the other cable.

TIP Seed beads are added as spacers and to make the beading cable less visible as the two strands weave between the glass beads and the pearls. A metallic finish or contrasting color to the other beads makes them a nice detailed accent.

5 Slide a fire-polished bead onto one strand, and once again pull the second cable through in the opposite direction. Pull on both cables to bring all the beads together. Repeat the alternating pattern of garnet beads with the seed bead/pearl/seed bead pattern until the bracelet reaches the length desired.

6 Make sure that the last bead is a fire-polished bead. Slide the tongue end of the clasp into the box and click in place. Slide a crimp bead onto one of the two cables. Pull the cable end through the corresponding loop on the tongue end of the clasp. Be sure that the beaded portion of the bracelet is not twisted, and that you choose the correct loop. Bring the cable back through the crimp bead, and pull in excess cable, forming a ³⁄₃₂" (2.4 mm) loop between the crimp bead and the clasp loop. Do not crimp the bead until you have repeated this step for the second cable, making it easier to adjust both cables and remove space between the beads before crimping them in place. Once adjusted, crimp the beads in place, and trim off the excess cable.

Variations

For earrings to match the bracelet, simply put two strands of cable together and crimp with a loop on the end. Add seed beads on each strand as spacers before you start the woven pattern that is on the bracelet. Add the beads as if you were doing one woven pattern, and then taper the strands with seed beads until they meet. Crimp a loop on the other end. Add an ear wire on one loop and a simple beaded drop on the other loop to finish your elegant earring.

Try a simple pattern with smaller 4mm and 6mm beads, varying the colors for a more delicate and colorful bracelet.

Once you have mastered this weaving method, adjust the number of edge beads to form a focal loop on a necklace.

WIRE:
Chandelier Earrings

There are many techniques for using wire in jewelry design; this chapter will explore some of the most basic methods for using a wire jig, as well as simple wire wrapping techniques with beads. With a wire jig, you can create your own components and connectors to customize your designs. This chandelier earring project introduces the wire jig, shows how to connect components, and how to embellish with beads. The variations explore different ways to use the same components, as well as other ways to use wire jig elements in your designs.

WHAT YOU'LL LEARN. . . . .

- How to use a wire jig to make unique components
- How to use nylon jaw pliers for your wire work

WHAT YOU'LL NEED. . . . .

TOOLS

- Round-nose pliers
- Chain-nose pliers
- Nylon jaw pliers
- Wire cutters
- Wire jig
- Ruler

MATERIALS

- 16" (40.6 cm) silver-tone wire (20 gauge)
- Eight 4 × 6mm pressed glass elongated beads: yellow
- Two 10 × 12mm pressed glass flat oval beads: yellow/brown stripe
- Four 4.5mm silver-tone jump rings (22 gauge)
- Two 4mm silver-tone ball posts with nuts
- Ten 1" (2.5 cm) silver-tone headpins

How to Make Chandelier Earrings

1 Pull the ***20 gauge wire*** through the nylon jaw pliers to remove any kinks. Cut the wire into four 4" (10.2 cm) pieces. Bend the end of one piece of wire into a ⅛" (3 mm) loop with round-nose pliers. Place four of the thinnest pegs into the ***wire jig*** base in a small square pattern, with one hole between each peg. Place the wire loop over one of the pegs, with the end of the wire facing the next peg in a counterclockwise direction.

2 Bring the wire around the side of the peg that is farther away from the first one, and wrap the wire around the peg clockwise, pulling the loop as snugly as you can around the peg.

3 Continuing to the third peg, wrap the wire around in a clockwise direction and press in place. Start to bring the wire around the fourth peg in a clockwise direction.

4 Wrap the wire once again in a clockwise direction around the fourth peg. Bring the wire around to the base of the fourth loop and carefully use chain-nose pliers to bend the remaining wire at a right angle to the base of the loop. Remove the wire from the wire jig; the side facing up is the top of your component.

5 With the top of the wire component facing up, grasp it gently with the nylon jaw pliers up to the base of the top loop where the excess wire remains. Use your fingers to wrap the wire around the base of the fourth loop, bringing it around the back, and to the front again. Use chain-nose pliers to make this wrap as tight as possible. Wrap the wire around to the back again.

TIP The wire may pull up on the pegs as you wrap it. After each loop, press the wire down toward the base of the jig using the side of the nylon jaw pliers. This will keep your design in place and will not mar the wire.

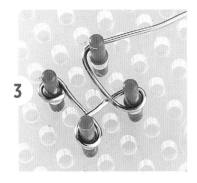

3

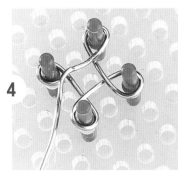

4

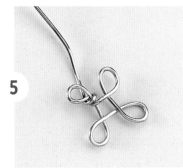

1

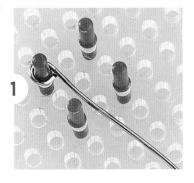

2

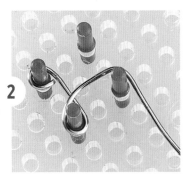

5

6 Clip the excess wire in the center back at the base of the loop. Gently press the end flat with chain-nose pliers. File or trim end more if necessary. Press the whole wire component flat with the nylon jaw pliers, being careful not to distort the shape, especially at the wrapped end. Repeat the steps to make a second component. For the other earring, make two more wire pieces, this time in the *reverse direction*. Open two silver jump rings. Attach the first wire piece with the wrapped loop at the top to the ball post loop with a jump ring. Close the ring. Attach the second wire piece with the wrapped loop at the top to the first with a second jump ring. Close the ring. Assemble the second earring the same way.

7 Place two oval beads and eight small yellow beads on headpins. Use round-nose pliers to make a ⅛" (3 mm) loop above each bead. Trim each loop.

8 Hook an oval bead onto the bottom loop of the bottom wire component and close the loop. Attach a small yellow bead to each of the four remaining loops on the sides of both wire pieces and close the loops. Repeat this step for the second earring.

6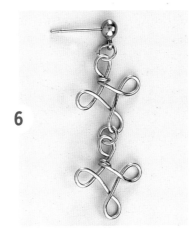

7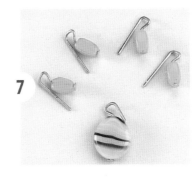

8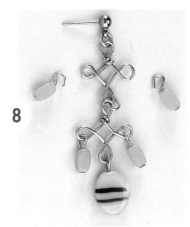

QUICK REFERENCE

20 gauge wire. The hardness or flexibility of wire varies depending on the type of metal, the gauge or thickness, and how much the wire has been manipulated. Wire will get stiffer as it gets worked more, and it can be partially hardened by flattening with nylon jaw pliers. You can use a nylon-faced hammer and a pad to better harden your wire elements; this will help them keep their shape. When using wire in jewelry components, select a gauge that is thick enough to support the piece you are constructing. If it is for decoration only, a thinner gauge can be used. All of the projects in this chapter use readily available permanently colored copper wire. You may also want to add a file to your tool kit for filing the trimmed wire ends.

Wire jig. For many wire projects made on a wire jig, you can work right off the spool, which will prevent waste. As you are first starting to work with wire, you may want to start with short pieces for ease of use.

Reverse direction. For the second earring, if you reverse the direction that you wrapped the wire for the first earring, your wraps will face in opposite directions, making a nicely balanced pair.

Variations

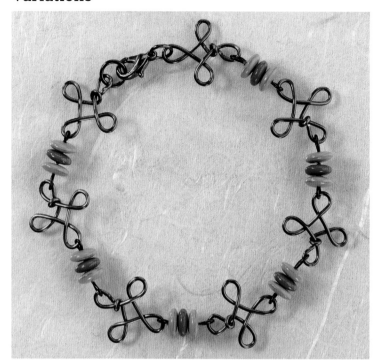

This bracelet uses the same wire components as the earring project, but in a copper colored wire. Instead of using jump rings to connect the wire pieces, they are attached with beads on eye pins.

The wire work on the round pendant started as a linear design on the wire jig. Beads were slid onto the wire before wrapping and added into the design during the wrapping. The linear pattern was then connected at the ends with a wire connector, and the inner part of the circle was formed with small beads on eye pins. The necklace is a braided finer gauge wire.

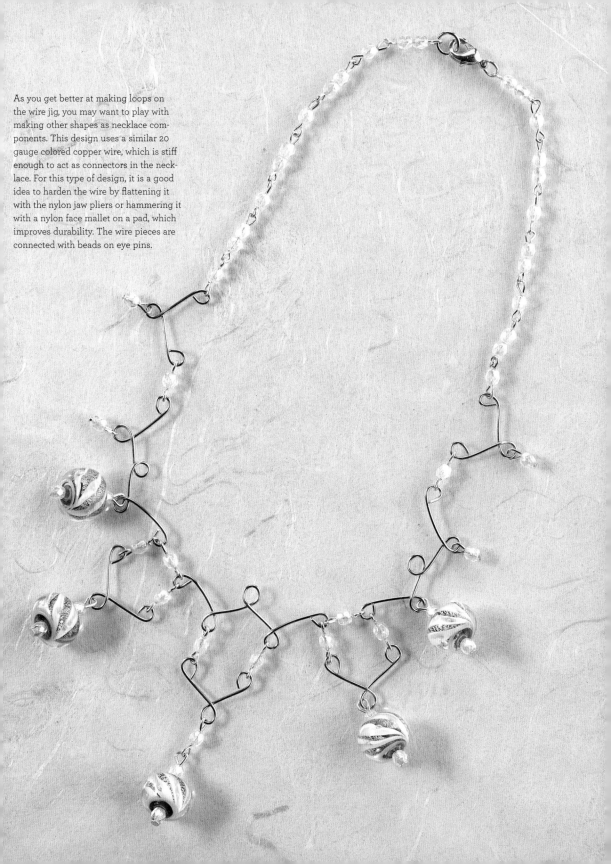

As you get better at making loops on the wire jig, you may want to play with making other shapes as necklace components. This design uses a similar 20 gauge colored copper wire, which is stiff enough to act as connectors in the necklace. For this type of design, it is a good idea to harden the wire by flattening it with the nylon jaw pliers or hammering it with a nylon face mallet on a pad, which improves durability. The wire pieces are connected with beads on eye pins.

WIRE:
Wrapped Shell Pendant

With this project you will learn some basic wire wrapping. Any doughnut-shaped jewelry component can be embellished using wire, and beads can be added as additional decoration. The wire can show as part of the design element or be completely covered in beads.

WHAT YOU'LL LEARN..

- How to do a simple wire wrap
- How to add beads as embellishment
- How to make a wire-wrapped loop

WHAT YOU'LL NEED..

TOOLS

- Chain-nose pliers
- Wire cutters
- Ruler

MATERIALS

- 3' (.9 m) silver-tone wire (24 gauge)
- Six rice-shaped freshwater pearls
- Seven potato-shaped freshwater pearls
- One doughnut-shaped shell

How to Make a Wrapped Shell Pendant

1 Cut a 2' (61 cm) long piece of wire. Slide one rice pearl onto one end, followed by one potato pearl. Continue to slide pearls onto the wire, alternating rice and potato pearls. You will have six rice pearls and five potato pearls on the wire.

TIP The length of the wire in these instructions is based on the width of the dough-nut; in this case the shell edge is ⅝" to ¾" (1.6 to 1.9 cm) wide. Adjust the wire length if your doughnut is wider or narrower.

2 Put the short end of the wire with pearls strung on it on it through the center of the shell doughnut and wrap it around the back. Wrap the long end with the pearls around to the back. Twist the two ends together and clip off the excess with the wire cutters. Make sure no sharp wire end is left protruding.

3 Begin to **wrap** by bringing the wire end back to the front of the doughnut through the center and wrap it back around to the back; there should now be two wire wraps showing on the front of the doughnut with no pearls on them. For the next wrap, bring the wire back through the center and slide a rice pearl onto that section of wire, positioning it close to the center of the doughnut. Wrap the wire back around and through

the center once again. Slide the next pearl (a potato pearl) onto this wrap, positioning it slightly more to the outer edge of the doughnut. Continue to wrap the shell, adding a pearl onto each wrap. After all of the pearls have been wrapped onto the shell, make two single wraps of wire without pearls. Finish the wire by twisting it with the previous wrap at the back of the doughnut and clipping off the excess.

4 Use the remaining section of wire and bend it to form a "U" shape. Slide a potato pearl onto each of the two ends and slide the pearls down close to the bend. Lay the "U" of wire with the bend at the top over the shell doughnut with the pearls lying on top of the shell. Wrap the two ends through the center of the doughnut to the back, and then pass the two ends through the bend in the wire, forming a ring hitch. Twist the two ends together and bend them around into a loop, wrapping the wire around the base of the loop to complete it. (See wire-wrapped loop on page 27.) A jump ring can be added to the loop to add the pendant to a chain.

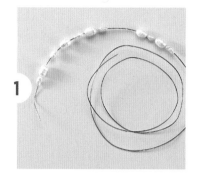

1

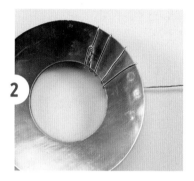

2

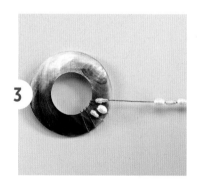

3

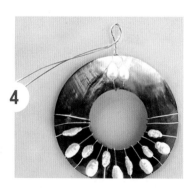

4

Variations

Try this same method and wire wrap two smaller shell loops for fun earrings. Three glass beads were added to each loop as embellishment.

For these earrings, seed beads were strung onto wire, which was then wrapped around the hoops. This method uses only the beads as an embellishment with no wire showing as part of the design. The hoops were wrapped in opposite directions to make mirror-image earrings.

Again using the same technique, jump rings can be wire wrapped onto a shell doughnut or loop to provide loops onto which drops can be attached. In this variation, five jump rings were added, glass drops on headpins were attached, and the matching glass beads were used in the chain and bead necklace portion of the piece.

QUICK REFERENCE

Wrap. Wire wrapped jewelry is often defined as the use of bundles of wires wrapped together in a decorative manner to create the framework or setting for stones, cabochons, or beads. The wire wrap in this chapter is a simple introduction to this technique.

WIRE:
Wired Bangle

With the previous project you did some basic wire wrapping. This bracelet will stretch your repertoire by showing you how to wrap wire in two directions. The bangle is decoratively wrapped in one direction and then the wired beads are applied as an embellishment running in a perpendicular direction to the first wire wrap.

WHAT YOU'LL LEARN . . . .

- How to wire wrap a bangle
- How to wrap wire in two different directions

WHAT YOU'LL NEED . . . .

TOOLS

- Chain-nose pliers
- Wire cutters
- Ruler

MATERIALS

- 6' (1.8 m) brown or copper wire (20 gauge)
- 2' (61 cm) orange wire (28 gauge)
- Fourteen $\frac{9}{16}$" × $\frac{3}{8}$" (1.4 × 1 cm) rectangular olive shell beads
- Black plastic bangle

How to Make a Wired Bangle

1 Cut a 6' (1.8 m) piece of brown wire. Hold the bangle with your left hand if right-handed (opposite for left-handed). Run the brown wire through the center of the bangle leaving a 3" (7.6 cm) piece of wire extending from the right side of the bangle. Hold the wire in place with your left hand and wrap the wire over the bangle from left to right and then back through the middle from right to left. Bring wire back around to the top. The wraps of brown wire will be about ⅜" (1 cm) apart.

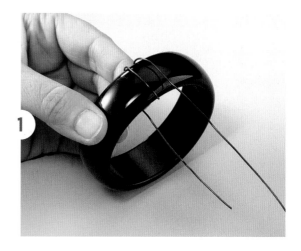

TIP The distance between the wraps will depend on the length of the beads you are using. The bead is attached at each end to a wire wrap with one wrap between, so the distance between wraps will be approximately one-half the length of your bead.

2 Cut a 2' (61 cm) piece of orange wire. Wrap the orange wire twice over the very first wrap of brown wire on the bangle. Leave a 2" (5.1 cm) section extending down from the brown wire.

3 Slide an olive shell bead onto the orange wire. Wrap the orange wire around the third brown wire wrap on the bangle. It is easiest to wrap the orange wire on before the brown wire has been passed back through the bangle. Once the orange wire has been secured, the brown wire can be wrapped back around the bangle as in step 1. Continue to add beads in the same manner all the way around the bangle. Once the bangle is complete, wrap the two ends of the orange wire together. Clip the excess, leaving ¼" (6 mm) of twisted wire, and tuck the wire end under a bead. Do the same with the two ends of the brown wire, tucking the twisted end under one of the beads.

TIP In this project you are wire-wrapping beads onto a flat or curved wire-wrapped surface. Because of this it is best to use flat or almost flat beads.

Variations

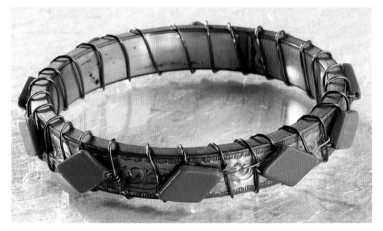

Try this same method with flat stone beads wired over a vintage gold bangle. The beads are spaced farther apart by adding an extra wrap around the bangle between beads and then wrapping the bead wire across without a bead on it. The end result is an entirely different look using the same technique.

A flat hoop was used for these earrings and beads were wired on in exactly the same manner as the bangle, with the beads facing toward the front of the hoop. Since the hoop had a hole for a center drop, a drop was added using two of the same beads placed on a headpin. The beads have an aurora borealis finish, and were flipped one with the AB side up and the next with the matte side up, giving the piece more visual interest.

This pendant has a mixture of beads wrapped onto it using the same technique as the flat beaded hoops. Spaces were left between the beads to allow the pattern of the base pendant to show through.

CHAIN:
Tassel Pendant

Chain is often used for hanging pendants, for connecting links or beads, or as a base for a bead or charm bracelet. This chapter explores decorative as well as functional applications for chain. This tassel pendant is made of simple strands of chain grouped together with a bead accent. The tassel works as a pendant, a purse charm, or a bauble for your cell phone or keys.

WHAT YOU'LL LEARN..

- How to combine chain strands to make a tassel
- How to mix two styles of chain for added texture
- How to use bead caps as functional elements of a design

WHAT YOU'LL NEED..

TOOLS

- Round-nose pliers
- Chain-nose pliers
- Wire cutters
- Ruler

MATERIALS

- 12" (30.5 cm) silver-tone figaro chain
- 12" (30.5 cm) silver-tone cable chain
- One 12 × 12mm flatted round lampwork bead: multicolored

- One 5 × 6mm silver-tone four-pointed bead cap (with a hole at each point)
- One 8mm silver-tone round, domed, flower-shaped bead cap with open looped edges
- Two 4mm silver-tone bead caps
- Two 1½" (3.8 cm) silver-tone eye pins
- Five 4.5mm silver-tone jump rings (22 gauge)
- One 12mm silver-tone lobster clasp

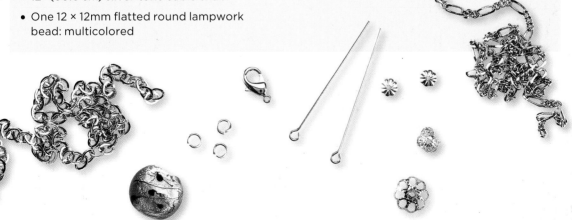

How to Make a Tassel Pendant

1 Bend one of the two eye pins in the center to form a "U" shape. Cut one 2¼" (5.7 cm) piece of the figaro chain. Hook one end of the chain onto the bent eye pin, and allow the chain to dangle straight down. Slide one end of the remaining long piece of chain onto the eye pin, next to the first piece, and cut the second piece to the same length as the first piece. Repeat this step until you have five equal lengths of the figaro chain. Remove the lengths and set aside, then repeat this step with the cable chain.

TIP By hooking the chain onto the eye pin and allowing gravity to work for you, it is easier to cut equal lengths of chain without having to measure each piece or count the links. With a figaro chain it is easy to count groups of links if you always start the chain at the same place in the link pattern, but with a small cable chain it is tedious to count links or try to measure each piece.

2 Open a jump ring and hook on one 2¼" (5.7 cm) piece of each of the two styles of chain. Slide the jump ring through the eye of the straight eye pin. Close the jump ring.

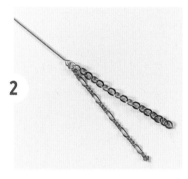

3 Slide the pointed cap onto the eye pin so that it covers the jump ring and top of the chain. Next, slide on the round, domed cap to cover the pointed cap. Add one of the small caps with the indentation of the cap facing away from the larger domed cap. Add the lamp-work bead, and then the final small cap. With round-nose pliers, form a loop at the top of the bead and cap, and cut off excess wire. Hook the wire through the hole on the clasp, and close the loop.

TIP Many lampwork beads have large holes, which will cause them to sit loosely on a standard head or eye pin. Adding a small cap to each end of the bead not only prevents wiggling on the eye pin, but also adds a nice detailed, decorative element. If you are forming a loop right next to a cap, make sure to close it tightly, or the cap may slide onto the loop.

4 To add the remaining chain, open a jump ring, and hook on one cut piece of figaro chain and one piece of cable chain. Hook the jump ring through one of the holes at one tip of the pointed cap, making sure the figaro chain faces to the outside of the tassel. Close the jump ring. Repeat this step until four jump rings with chain have been added to complete the tassel.

Variations

These fun, textured earrings use much of the same construction as the tassel pendant. Eliminating the domed cap makes the jump rings a decorative part of the design. Each chain strand is accented with a bead drop, adding fullness to the tassels.

Simple folded-over sections of chain create a tassel look. The graduated lengths make an attractive cascade when attached to a loop and connector base chain with delicate beads. This shows both functional and decorative applications of chain, with beads added for color.

The folded-over sections of chain between each bead on this bracelet form mini-tassels for a cascading bracelet with a lot of movement.

CHAIN:
Draped Chain Earrings

The tassel pendant project and variations on page 125 illustrated different ways to use straight strands of chain to create decorative tassels and fringe. Take this in a new direction by attaching both ends of chain to the base piece of jewelry, forming swags. This project combines necklace ends, chain, and bead drops for a very elegant yet simple earring.

WHAT YOU'LL LEARN . . . .

- How to form multiple swags with chain
- How to use necklace ends as decorative earring parts
- How to add bead caps to coordinate beaded elements with metal parts

WHAT YOU'LL NEED . . . .

TOOLS

- Round-nose pliers
- Chain-nose pliers
- Wire cutters
- Ruler

MATERIALS

- 16" (40.6 cm) gold-tone small cable chain
- Two 6 × 8mm Czech glass fire-polished teardrop beads: green iris

- Two 4mm Czech glass fire-polished beads: green iris
- Eight 4.5mm gold-tone jump rings (22 gauge)
- Two gold-tone lever-back wires
- Two gold-tone decorative three-strand necklace ends
- Two 1" (2.5 cm) gold-tone headpins
- Two 4mm gold-tone bead caps
- Two 2.5mm gold-tone bead caps

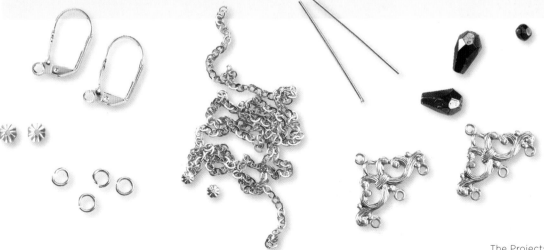

How to Make Draped Chain Earrings

1 Use chain-nose pliers to open all eight jump rings. Hook one open jump ring through one of the two outside loops on one of the necklace ends. Close the loop. Hook a second jump ring on the other outside loop of the necklace end and close the ring. Repeat this step for the second necklace end.

2 Measure one 3" (7.6 cm) strand of the small linked chain and cut. Hook one end of the chain onto the hook portion of one of the lever-back wires, and allow the chain to dangle straight down. Slide one end of the remaining long piece of chain onto the lever-back wire, next to the first piece, and cut the second piece to the same length as the first piece. Remove the chain from the lever-back wire and set aside.

3 Repeat step 2 to cut two pieces of chain that are 2½" (6.4 cm) long, and two pieces of chain that are 2" (5.1 cm) long.

4 Hook one 3" (7.6 cm) piece of chain, one 2½" (6.4 cm) piece of chain, and one 2" (5.1 cm) piece of chain onto one open jump ring. Hook the jump ring through one of the jump rings already attached to one of the necklace ends. Make sure that the longest chain is hanging to the outside of the loop and necklace end, and the shortest chain hangs to the inside. Close the ring.

TIP When attaching graduated chain lengths, it is easiest to use gravity to determine if the chains are attached properly. Hook the jump ring with chains onto the necklace end, close the loop, and hold up the necklace end to make sure the chains are in order.

1

2

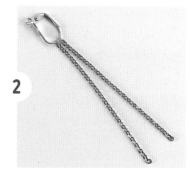

3

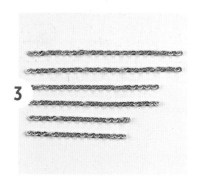

4

QUICK REFERENCE

Swags of chain create a beautiful, vintage look on earrings and necklaces. While constructing the swags, you may need to add extra jump rings in order to get the swags to sit flat when viewed from the front. For this project, because of the loops that already exist on the necklace ends, two jump rings are needed on each side of the swag instead of one. If you used only one set of jump rings, the three separate strands of chain would stack on top of each other when viewed from the front, which would create a completely different look.

5 To make the **swags**, hook an open jump ring first through the end of the shortest chain, and then the medium chain, and then the longest chain. Hook the jump ring through the jump ring that is already attached on the opposite end of the necklace end. Close the ring. Hold the necklace end to make sure that the chain hangs properly and that the chains are not twisted. You may need to reverse the jump ring to get the swags of chain to sit flat. Repeat steps 4 and 5 to make the swags on the second earring.

6 To make the drops, slide a 4mm cap onto a headpin with the curve facing up. Slide on a teardrop bead, and then add the tiny cap so it wraps around to top of the teardrop. Add the 4mm bead and use round nose pliers to form a ⅛" (3 mm) loop at the top of the bead. Trim any excess wire. Repeat this step to make the second drop.

TIP Metal bead caps added to a beaded drop can tie in the drop with the metal chain and necklace end details on the earring. When putting caps on teardrops, make sure to choose a size that does not extend past the top and the bottom of the bead. This is especially important when putting caps on beaded drops on necklaces, as oversized caps will rub against the skin, or may catch in your hair or clothing.

7 Hang one of the beaded drops off the center loop on one of the necklace ends with the chain swags. Close the loop on the drop. Open the loop on one of the lever-back wires and hook the top loop of the necklace end onto the lever-back wire. Close the loop. Repeat this step to finish the second earring.

5

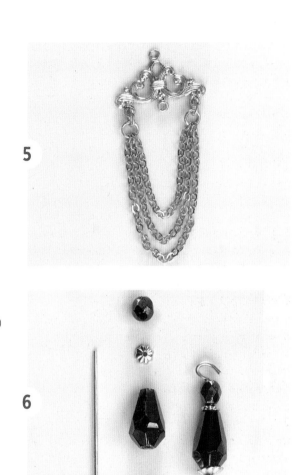

6

7

Variations

Try attaching chains from the end loops to the center loop on the necklace ends for a double set of swags, accented by a beaded tassel in the center. This may be a little tricky to assemble, but makes for a dramatic earring.

To make this necklace, cut graduated swags of chain in advance. Place a crimp on one end of the beading cable and string the necklace from the center to one end. This is the easiest way to get the spacing for the chain to work out, as well as the correct length of the necklace. Once one side is beaded, you can add the clasp and string the second half.

Although it is difficult to see the swags on the bracelet, the graduated lengths of bar chain on this piece add fullness and movement that you would not get from using equal lengths of chain.

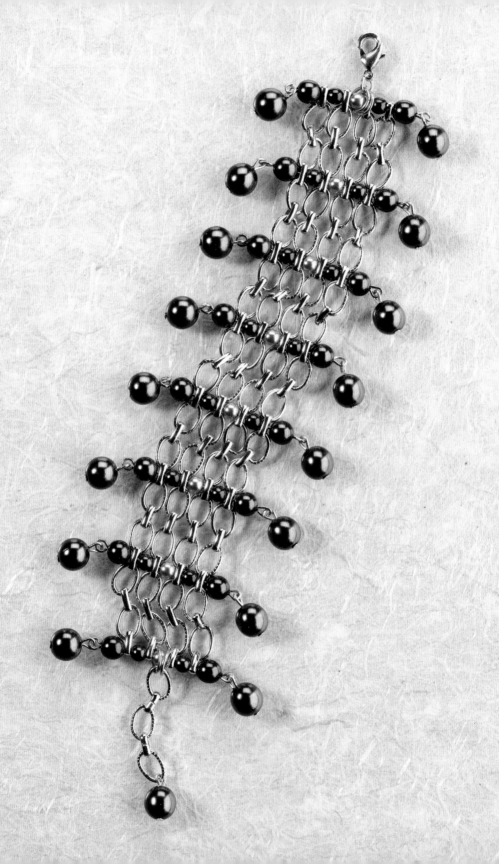

CHAIN:
Chain Mesh Bracelet

Chain comes in many styles and sizes, which makes it easy to vary the scale and texture of your pieces. This chain mesh bracelet takes advantage of the built-in connectors in a medium-sized loop and connector chain. This repetitive element combined with beaded eye pins and beaded drops uses several of the skills you have learned.

WHAT YOU'LL LEARN...

- How to maximize the functional and decorative aspects of chain
- How to connect multiple strands of chain with beads and eye pins to create mesh
- How to graduate the color and size of beads for visual impact
- How to make a bracelet extender for size adjustment

WHAT YOU'LL NEED...

TOOLS

- Round-nose pliers
- Chain-nose pliers
- Wire cutters
- Ruler

MATERIALS

- 29" (73.7 cm) gold-tone medium sized oval loop and connector chain
- Seventeen 8mm glass pearls: brown

- Sixteen 6mm glass pearls: brown
- Sixteen 4mm glass pearls: brown
- Eight 4mm glass pearls: copper
- Four 6mm gold-tone jump rings (20 gauge)
- One 4.5mm gold-tone jump ring (22 gauge)
- Seventeen 1" (2.5 cm) gold-tone headpins
- Eight 2" (5.1 cm) gold-tone eye pins
- One 12mm gold-tone lobster clasp

How to Make a Chain Mesh Bracelet

1

2

1 Cut a piece of loop and connector chain that has three loops and two connectors. Open two of the 6mm jump rings and attach them to one end of this short piece of chain. Close the loops. Slide an 8mm brown pearl onto a headpin, make a ⅛" (3 mm) loop, and trim the excess wire. Hook the drop onto the other end of the short piece of chain to complete your bracelet extender. Close the other two 6mm jump rings. Open the 4.5mm jump ring and slide it through the loop on the clasp. Add the two 6mm closed jump rings, and then close the smaller jump ring. The clasp and extender are ready for the bracelet.

2 Measure a 6¼" to 6¾" (15.9–17.2 cm) piece of loop and connector chain. Make sure that the chain starts and ends with a connector, and that there is an even number of loops. Cut three more strands that are the same length. Remove the chain lengths and set aside.

TIP Loop and connector chains will vary. Measure the bracelet length, minus the clasp, and cut the chain accordingly. You may need to adjust the length of the chain slightly to get connectors on both ends plus an even number of loops. It is better to cut the chain slightly shorter than necessary rather than longer, since the bracelet will have an extender for an adjustable closure. Make sure that the loops on your chain are large yet thin enough for the clasp to hook over on the extender.

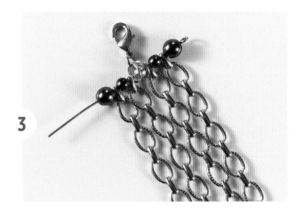

3

3 Slide a 6mm brown pearl onto one eye pin. Slide the eye pin through the first connector loop on the end of one cut piece of chain. Add a 4mm brown pearl, and then slide the eye pin through the first connector loop on the second piece of chain. Slide the eye pin through the first 6mm closed jump ring attached to the clasp, add a 4mm copper pearl onto the eye pin, and then slide the eye pin through the second 6mm closed jump ring attached to the clasp. Slide the eye pin through the first connector loop on the third piece of chain, and then add a 4mm brown pearl. Finally, slide the eye pin through the first connector loop on the fourth piece of chain, and then add a 6mm brown pearl. Make a ⅛" (3 mm) loop just after the last pearl, trim the excess wire, and close the loop.

4 Slide a 6mm brown pearl onto an eye pin. On the end opposite the clasp, slide the eye pin through the first connector loop on the end of one cut piece of chain. Add a 4mm brown pearl, and then slide the eye pin through the first connector loop on the second piece of chain. Slide the eye pin through the first 6mm closed jump ring attached to the extender, add a 4mm copper pearl onto the eye pin, and then slide the eye pin through the second 6mm closed jump ring attached to the extender. Slide the eye pin through the first connector loop on the third piece of chain, and then add a 4mm brown pearl. Finally, slide the eye pin through the first connector loop on the fourth piece of chain, and then add a 6mm brown pearl. Make a ⅛" (3 mm) loop just after the last pearl, cut excess wire, and close the loop.

TIP Make sure to add the chain onto the eye pin in the same order on both the clasp and the extender end of the bracelet so that it lies flat and starts to look like mesh.

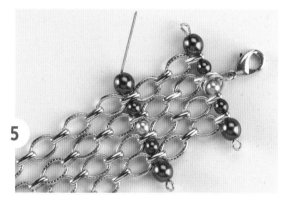

5 Working again at the clasp end of the brace-let, skip the first set of connector loops that are already connected with beads and eye pin, and go to the third set of connector loops. Use the same beading pattern as you did on the ends of the bracelet, always sliding the eye pin through the corresponding connector on the second third and fourth chains: onto an eye pin slide on a 6mm brown pearl, the third connector loop of the first chain, a 4mm brown pearl, the third connector loop of the second chain, a 4mm copper pearl, the third connector loop of the third chain, a 4mm brown pearl, the third connector loop of the fourth chain, and a 6mm brown pearl. Once you have completed this pattern, make a loop, trim the excess wire, and close the loop. Repeat this beading pattern on every other set of connector loops until you reach the extender end of the bracelet.

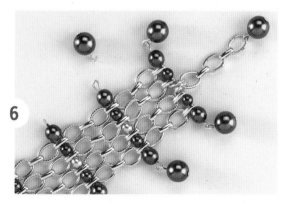

6 Slide a 6mm brown pearl onto a headpin. Make a ⅛" (3 mm) loop, and trim the excess wire. Repeat this step until you have sixteen drops prepared. Add a 6mm brown pearl drop to each of the end loops of the eye pins to complete the bracelet.

Variations

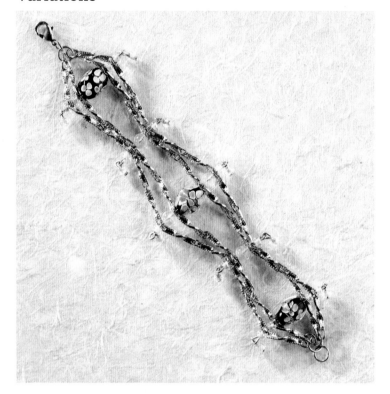

For a completely different twist on the same style of bracelet, this example uses a twisted bar chain and varies the number of beads on the eye pin connectors, creating an undulating effect that is angular and does not look like mesh.

For the earrings, the chain was connected with an eye pin only on one end, leaving the graduated beaded strand of chain to hang free, combining the mesh technique with the fringe look explored in the tassel project variations (page 125).

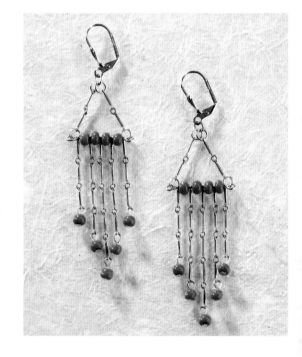

This textural necklace maximizes the combination of functional and decorative uses of chain. Mesh segments made from multiple strands of chain linked by beaded eye pins are broken up with chain connectors to accent beads, and culminate in a fringed chain cascade. As you work more with chain and construction, you will find many unique ways to construct jewelry by combining techniques.

MEMORY WIRE:
Triple-Loop Earrings

Memory wire is a tempered stainless steel beading wire that comes in several different sizes for making rings, bracelets, anklets, and necklaces. It is an easy material to work with, as the fact that it permanently holds its shape, even while being flexible, eliminates the need for clasps on many designs. The projects in this chapter use three different sizes of the memory wire to stimulate a variety of ideas of how to use this fun beading material. Although the first project uses the ring-sized wire, the unexpected result is a high-impact pair of earrings.

WHAT YOU'LL LEARN . . . .

- How to make end loops on memory wire
- How to use ring-sized memory wire to create jewelry components
- How to finish the end of beaded memory wire

WHAT YOU'LL NEED . . . .

TOOLS

- Chain-nose pliers
- Round-nose pliers
- Heavy-duty wire cutters

MATERIALS

- Nine coils of ring-sized memory wire
- Forty-five to fifty 4mm Austrian or Czech bicone crystal beads: crystal AB
- Two silver-tone French ear wires
- Four 4mm silver-tone jump rings (22 gauge)

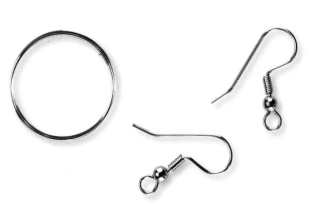

How to Make Triple Loop Earrings

1 Cut a single coil of *memory wire* plus ½" (1.3 cm) using the heavy-duty wire cutters. Cut five more of these loops. You will use three loops for each earring. Use round-nose pliers to bend a closed loop on one end of one of the coils. Repeat this step for two more loops of wire.

2 Slide fifteen to seventeen crystals onto the first loop of wire. Leave about ¼" (6 mm) of the wire free of beads. Very carefully form a loop at this end of the wire.

TIP You may need to vary the number of crystals on the loop to accommodate the differences in bead or memory wire sizes. Make sure to leave enough unbeaded wire at the end to make a complete loop without cracking the last crystal or making the beading so tight that it distorts the shape of the loop.

3 Slide seven to eight crystals onto the second loop of wire. Once the beads go halfway (not including the extra length of wire added for the second loop), slide the straight end of the second wire through both end loops on the first beaded loop.

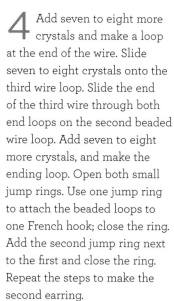

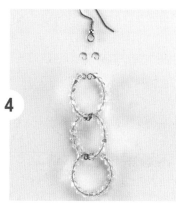

4 Add seven to eight more crystals and make a loop at the end of the wire. Slide seven to eight crystals onto the third wire loop. Slide the end of the third wire through both end loops on the second beaded wire loop. Add seven to eight more crystals, and make the ending loop. Open both small jump rings. Use one jump ring to attach the beaded loops to one French hook; close the ring. Add the second jump ring next to the first and close the ring. Repeat the steps to make the second earring.

QUICK REFERENCE

Memory wire comes in coiled stacks that look like a Slinky or a spring. The wire can be cut to custom lengths depending on how many loops you need for your design. If you make a design with single loop elements such as these earrings, make sure to cut the coil with a ¼" to ⅜" (6 mm to 1 cm) overlap to accommodate the extra length needed for end loops. For a bracelet, you may need to add more to make a double loop on each end so you can add decorative drops.

Variations

Add drops to a single beaded loop for a fun chandelier hoop earring. It may take a few tries on the beading to get the drops centered.

Use seed beads on a double loop of memory wire to create a simple ring base. Larger beads will make the ring bulky, so use small beads unless you need the extra bulk to make the ring smaller. Add a larger jump ring through the two end loops, and five smaller jump rings to the large one. This will give you enough space to add five drops to each of the small jump rings for this "shooting star" ring.

This necklace expands upon the concept of making beaded loop jewelry components like the earring project. The memory wire has enough rigidity to maintain its shape even as necklace elements, and can easily be connected together to form a chain with a combination of jump rings and beaded eye pins.

MEMORY WIRE:
Heart Choker

In this project you will be using the necklace size memory wire which, when completed, sits around the neck like a choker. The springy nature of the wire allows the choker to sit comfortably without needing a clasp. Chokers made with memory wire can be made by stringing beads directly onto the wire and can then be embellished by adding beaded drops, chain, or charms. One thing to keep in mind is not to use beads that are excessively large or heavy as these may make the necklace fall off. If you want to use large or heavy beads, add a clasp at the back of the choker by attaching jump rings to the loops in the memory wire

WHAT YOU'LL LEARN..

- How to use necklace memory wire
- How to add drops to a simple choker
- How to bead the choker by starting in the middle

WHAT YOU'LL NEED..

TOOLS

- Chain-nose pliers
- Round-nose pliers
- Wire cutters
- Heavy-duty wire cutters
- Ruler
- Clear tape

MATERIALS

- 16" (40.6 cm) necklace memory wire
- Nine peach glass hearts in graduated sizes: one 15mm, two 10mm, two 8mm, four 6mm
- One hundred twenty 4mm faceted Czech glass beads: peach
- Seven 2" (5.1 cm) gold-tone headpins

How to Make a Heart Choker

1 Use heavy-duty wire cutters to cut a 16" (40.6 cm) piece of necklace size memory wire; this is approximately a coil and a half of the wire.

2 Slide the 15mm heart on one of the gold headpins followed by three 4mm peach beads. Turn over the top of the headpin to form a loop, trim the excess and close the loop. Place one of the 10mm hearts onto a headpin, add two 4mm beads and finish a ⅛" loop at the top. Repeat with the other 10mm bead. Place one of the 8mm beads on a headpin, add two 4mm beads and finish the loop; repeat with the other 8mm heart bead. Place one of the 6mm heart beads on a headpin, add two 4mm beads, finish loop; repeat with another 6mm heart. Place each of the last two 6mm hearts onto the last two headpins and add one 4mm bead onto each headpin. Form a loop with the pliers, trim the excess, but do not close the loop on the final two hearts.

3 To keep the design symmetrical sometimes it is easier to start in the middle of a necklace or choker. Slide the drop with the 15mm heart onto the center of the wire. Slide three 4mm Czech glass beads onto the wire on either side of the center drop. Slide a 10mm heart drop onto each side of the choker, followed by three more 4mm beads.

4 Add an 8mm heart drop onto each side of the choker followed by three 4mm peach glass beads on each side. Add a 6mm heart drop onto each side; this is the final drop on each side. To ensure that the beads already on the memory wire do not slide off, place a small piece of clear tape around one end of the choker wire, then add forty 4mm beads to the other end. Turn the wire end into a double loop using round-nose pliers. Remove the tape, place forty beads on the other side of the choker, and finish the end in the same manner. Attach the remaining two heart drops to the two loops at the ends of the choker and close the loops of the drops using chain-nose pliers.

TIP Because memory wire is made from tempered stainless steel, it is important to use heavy-duty wire cutters; it will damage regular wire cutters.

1

2

3

4

Variations

In this variation, the beaded drops are replaced by heart charms and the beaded portion of the choker has been accentuated by using a slight variation of beads in addition to the 4mm faceted Czech glass.

Beading the necklace size memory wire with the same bead all the way around makes it an excellent backdrop from which to hang any pendant. This variation uses 4mm amethyst Czech glass with 8mm beads at the ends. Attached is a polymer clay heart pendant.

This memory wire choker was beaded with much larger beads to show the difference in scale. It is kept simple with no additional drops or charms added. This is a quick and easy way to make a great accessory.

MEMORY WIRE:
Memory Wire Bracelet

Bracelets in particular lend themselves to multi-coil designs, and for this project you will make a two-strand bracelet. You could easily change the design and make a more substantial design statement with more coils. The springy nature of the wire allows the bracelet to sit comfortably and be wrapped around the arm without needing a clasp. Many craft stores sell mixed bags of similar-colored beads, and this project can easily be made using one of those mixes.

WHAT YOU'LL LEARN..

- How to use bracelet memory wire
- How to use beads randomly, but in a pattern
- How to finish memory wire ends

WHAT YOU'LL NEED..

TOOLS

- Chain-nose pliers
- Round-nose pliers
- Wire cutters
- Heavy-duty wire cutters
- Ruler

MATERIALS

- Two and one-half coils bracelet memory wire
- Sixty-five 4 to 6mm random turquoise color beads
- Eleven 9 to 15mm turquoise, white, or patterned beads
- Two 2″ (5.1 cm) silver-tone headpins

How to Make a Memory Wire Bracelet

1 Use heavy-duty wire cutters to cut two and one-half coils of bracelet memory wire. You will need about 1" (2.5 cm) of memory wire at each end of the bracelet to form the finishing loop, therefore two and one-half coils of wire is required to make a double coil bracelet.

TIP Memory wire is available in both a standard bracelet size and a large bracelet size. The standard bracelet size is used for this project, and it will make a bracelet that fits snugly around the wrist. The standard bracelet size is generally better for use with smaller beads. If larger beads are being used or if you would like a bracelet with more of a bangle type fit, use the large bracelet size wire.

2 Use round-nose pliers to form a double loop on one end of the memory wire. Make sure that the cut end does not protrude in a manner that may scratch the wearer.

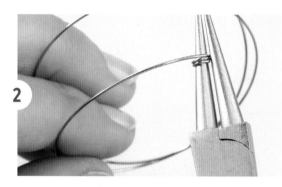

3 The beading pattern for this bracelet is five small beads followed by one of the larger beads. Slide five of the smaller turquoise beads onto the unfinished end of the memory wire. The beads can be selected randomly. Follow the five beads with a larger turquoise bead. Slide five more of the small beads onto the wire followed by a patterned turquoise bead. Add five smaller beads followed by a patterned white bead. Continue this pattern until only about 1" (2.5 cm) of the wire remains at the end. Finish the end as in step 2.

4 Slide two of the smaller turquoise beads onto one of the headpins. Form a loop above the beads and cut off the excess. Close the loop over a loop at one end of the memory wire. Repeat for the other end of the bracelet.

Variations

In this variation three and one-half coils of memory wire were used. The beading pattern is six seed beads followed by a wood bead.

Memory wire bracelets can also be embellished using beaded drops. This fun bracelet is beaded with 4mm faceted glass beads interspersed with beaded drops.

Memory wire can also be used with beads that have two holes. This flowery cuff is made using two pieces that are each one and one-half coils run through a series of double-holed beads.

FILIGREE:
Filigree Post Earrings

There is an endless array of parts and findings that can be used in beaded jewelry; the challenge is deciding what you like. This chapter focuses on filigree. Filigree can be a beautiful, detailed, structural part of jewelry design, perfect for creating vintage looks. It is simple to use and the open work in the metal is convenient for adding drops and attaching elements. The filigree post earring project introduces you to layering filigree and adding a bead detail.

WHAT YOU'LL LEARN...........

- How to use filigree as another decorative component of beaded jewelry
- How to glue filigree
- How to place an earring post

WHAT YOU'LL NEED...........

TOOLS

- Wooden skewer or toothpick
- Piece of paper

MATERIALS

- Two 4mm ivory glass pearls
- Two ⅞" × 1⅛" (2.2 × 2.9 cm) antique gold-tone oval filigrees
- Two ¾" (1.9 cm) antique silver-tone lacy round filigrees
- Two ⅝" (1.6 cm) gold-tone round filigrees
- Two 10mm flat pad posts with earring nuts with plastic flange
- Rub 'n Buff metallic finish (optional)
- E-6000 industrial craft glue

How to Make Filigree Post Earrings

1 Using a toothpick or skewer, spread a coat of **E-6000 glue** on the center surface of one antique gold oval **filigree**. Place a silver round filigree on the glue and center on the oval filigree. Repeat this step for the second earring.

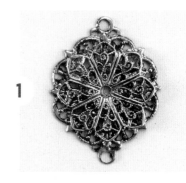

2 Spread a coat of glue in the center of the round silver filigree. Center the small round gold filigree on top. Repeat this step for the second earring.

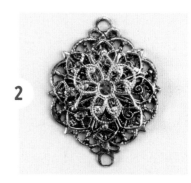

3 With a toothpick, place a dab of glue on the back of a pearl. Center the pearl over the stacked filigrees and press in place. Repeat for the second earring. Allow the glue to dry.

TIP Since you are using a bead with a hole for the center decoration, try to align the hole so that it is the least visible. Setting the bead on its side with the hole running from top to bottom, parallel to the surface of the filigree, will look the best.

4 With a toothpick, place a dab of glue just above the center of the filigree on the back of one earring. Press a post in place. Repeat for the second earring.

TIP When making medium-sized or larger post earrings, glue the post above the center of the earring back, and wear it with a nut that has a plastic disk or flange. Both of these steps will help the post sit flat on the ear and prevent it from drooping.

QUICK REFERENCE

E-6000 glue is an industrial strength glue that is good for gluing metal components. Read the precautions on the label, as it should be used in a well-ventilated area. Always use a fresh dab of glue straight out of the tube for each step, for the best results.

Filigrees are available in many shapes, sizes, and finishes. If you can't find the finish you want, you can always add an antiqued look or a colored patina by coating the filigree with Rub 'n Buff, a wax-based metallic finish. Simply follow the manufacturer's instructions.

Variations

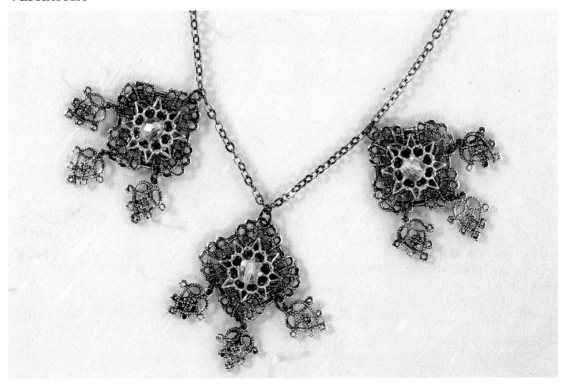

For a simple yet elegant vintage style necklace, combine different antiqued filigrees, subtle colored beads, and use small filigrees as drops. Hang the pieces from a gunmetal chain, and you have an instant heirloom.

For these filigree drop earrings, use the edge loops to connect two layered, beaded filigrees, then attach them to a hook.

You can also make beautiful hair accessories by layering larger filigrees. For added detail, this hair clip is dotted with seed beads and enhanced with a double swag of chain.

FILIGREE:
Filigree and Bead Bracelet

Filigree can be turned in any direction in a design and bead drops on headpins can be added to any of the open loops. In this project, multiples of the same filigree are attached together to form a bracelet, and the beaded drops are attached to the filigree loops along the edges for embellishment.

WHAT YOU'LL LEARN...

- How to attach filigrees together to form a bracelet
- How to attach drops to filigree
- How to use beaded drops to embellish filigree

WHAT YOU'LL NEED...

TOOLS

- Chain-nose pliers
- Wire cutters

MATERIALS

- Sixteen 6mm bicone glass beads: copper
- Sixteen 6mm bicone glass beads: light gray

- Thirty-two 1" (2.5 cm) silver-tone headpins
- Eight ¾" (1.9 cm) silver-tone oval filigrees
- Eight 4mm silver-tone jump rings (22 gauge)
- One 6.5mm silver-tone jump ring (20 gauge)
- One 12mm silver-tone lobster clasp

How to Make a Filigree and Bead Bracelet

1 Slide a copper bicone bead onto one of the headpins. Make a loop above the bead, trim the excess with the wire cutters, and attach the loop to one of the openings to the side of the center of a filigree. Repeat with the other three copper beads, attaching four drops total to the filigree. Add copper beads in the same manner to three additional filigrees.

TIP The finished length of this bracelet is 7¼" (18.4 cm). If you need the bracelet to be longer, add another filigree to the design, and if you need the bracelet to be shorter, subtract one. If you need more adjustment in the length, you can also add larger (6.5mm) jump rings to the end without the clasp so that the bracelet becomes adjustable.

2 Slide a gray bead onto one of the headpins. Make a loop above the bead, trim the excess with the wire cutters, and attach the loop to one of the openings to the side of the center of a filigree. Repeat with the other three gray beads, attaching four drops total to the filigree. Add gray beads in the same manner to three additional filigrees.

3 Place a filigree with copper beads and a filigree with gray beads right sides together and attach the two filigrees together by running a 4mm silver-tone jump ring through the loops at one end of each filigree. Continue to attach all of the filigrees together, alternating the filigrees with copper drops and the filigrees with gray drops.

4 Once all eight of the filigrees are connected, attach the 6.5mm jump ring to the loop of the filigree at one end of the bracelet and attach the clasp to the other end using a 4mm jump ring.

1

2

3

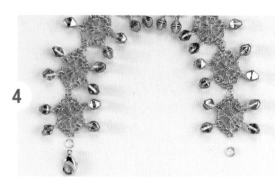

4

Variations

Filigree is great to use for earrings. The openings in the filigree designs allow for multiple drops to be attached as shown in this fun pair of earrings.

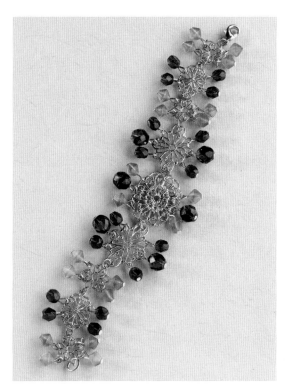

In this variation, two filigrees were attached together to form a pendant, and then a variety of drops were added.

This bracelet is similar to the project bracelet, however multiple types of filigree in graduating sizes were used, with the largest in the center and tapering off on the sides. Drops were added to the sides in a similar manner as the project.

FILIGREE:
Embellished Filigree Brooch

This brooch project combines filigree techniques learned in previous projects and adds the concept of enhancing the edges of the filigree by wrapping beads on with wire. The prominent center filigree is accented with a colored metallic finish. By combining all of these elements, the result is an ornate brooch with rich detailing.

WHAT YOU'LL LEARN . . . .

- How to add color to filigree as an additional design element
- How to create a beaded flower accent
- How to wire wrap beads onto the edge of filigree
- How to attach a pin back

WHAT YOU'LL NEED . . . .

TOOLS

- Round-nose pliers
- Chain-nose pliers
- Wire cutters
- Wooden skewer or toothpick

MATERIALS

- 14" (35.6 cm) gold-tone wire (24 gauge)
- Four 12mm round Indian glass fiorato style beads: aqua green
- Seventeen e-beads: cinnamon (number will vary depending on edge design of round filigree)
- Four 6mm Czech fire-polished beads: aqua opal

- Eleven or twelve 4mm Czech fire-polished beads: aqua opal (number depends on size of center bead)
- One 2" (5.1 cm) square gold-tone filigree with indented (dapped) center
- One 2" (5.1 cm) pin back
- Six 5mm gold-tone bead caps
- Seven 1" (2.5 cm) gold-tone headpins
- One 1½" (3.8 cm) gold-tone round filigree with indented (dapped) center
- Rub 'n Buff® metallic wax finish: Chinese red
- E-6000 industrial craft glue
- Paper towel

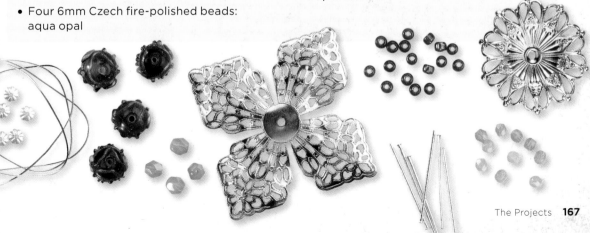

How to Make an Embellished Filigree Brooch

1 To **glue the pin back**, use a toothpick with a pea-sized bead of **E-6000 glue** (pg. 152) to make a line down the center of the back of the square filigree. Place the pin back with the hinged end toward the top tip of the square in the line of glue. Press in place and allow the glue to dry.

2 Place a bead cap with the indentation facing up on a headpin. Add one Indian glass **fiorato bead**, another cap that cups over the top of the bead, and an e-bead. Make a ⅛" (3 mm) loop at the top and trim excess wire. Repeat this to make two other fiorato drops, and then make four drops that have a 6mm aqua fire-polished bead and an e-bead. Make loops on all the drops and trim excess wire.

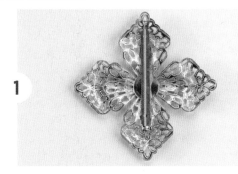

3 Double check to see which corner of the square filigree is the top, based on the pin back placement, before you attach the drops. Attach one fiorato bead drop to the bottom center loop of the square filigree and close the loop. Add a 6mm aqua bead drop on each side, closing the loops. Attach a fiorato bead drop on each bottom side of the square filigree, so that they are balanced. Close the loops. Add an aqua 6mm bead drop to the outside of each of the side fiorato drops, and close the loops.

4 To prepare the round **dapped** filigree, use a paper towel to apply a small amount of the Rub 'n Buff® metallic finish to the entire surface. Wipe off the excess, leaving the color in the textured indentations of the filigree. Allow the filigree to dry. Cut a 10" (25.4 cm) piece of wire and pull it from the bottom of the filigree through to the front, leaving a 1" (2.5 cm) tail in the back. Slide on an e-bead, wrap the wire around the edge of the filigree to the back side, and pull the wire back up through one of the holes on the edge. Add another e-bead and wrap the wire around. Use the design on the edge of the filigree to determine the spacing and number of beads you add to the edge.

5 Once you have added the final e-bead to the edge of the filigree, wrap the wire around to the back side. Twist the two ends of the wire together, trim the twist to 3/16" (5 mm), and bend until it is flat against the back of the filigree.

6 Place the remaining fiorato bead on its side on your work surface. Slide eleven 4mm aqua beads onto the remaining 4" (10.2 cm) piece of wire. Wrap the beaded wire around the fiorato bead to check for gaps or if additional beads are needed. The 4mm beads should just fit around the edge of the larger bead. Twist the ends of the wire together and trim the twist to 3/16" (5 mm), bending it toward the center of the bead loop, parallel to the surface of the loop.

7 Spread a layer of glue in the center of the indentation on the round filigree. Place the beaded loop in the glue and gently press into place. Add a dab of glue to the back of the fiorato bead and press it into the center of the beaded loop. Since you do not want to see the hole, make sure the fiorato bead is on its side, with the hole running parallel to the surface of the filigree. Spread a pea-sized dab of glue in the center of the square filigree. Place the round filigree on top and press it into place, aligning the round filigree as you desire. Allow the brooch to dry on a level surface.

QUICK REFERENCE

Glue pin back. You have the option of gluing a pin back on either vertically or horizontally. This design would make an excellent dramatic pendant as well, so it is a good idea to attach the pin back vertically, with the hinged part of the pin very close to the top center of the filigree. This way, it can easily be hooked over a chain or ribbon and worn as a pendant, giving the brooch additional versatility.

A **fiorato bead** is based originally on an Italian style glass bead with flowers.

Dapping is a method used to press an indentation into a metal piece such as filigree to give it dimension, either convex or concave. Selecting a dapped filigree for the centerpiece on this brooch allows you to have the extra space to wire beads on the edge, and adds more depth to the finished piece.

6

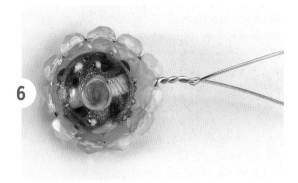

5

7

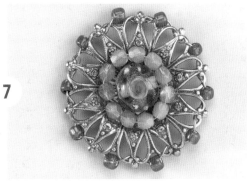

Variations

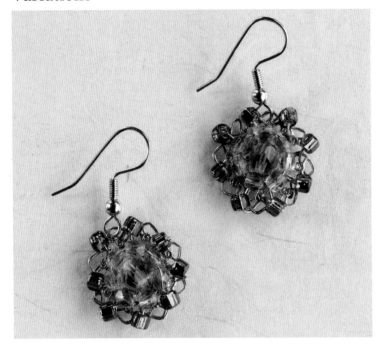

Add a wired, beaded edge and a beaded flower to a pair of simple, round filigrees for instant drop earrings.

Color enhanced hoop filigrees look exotic when beaded with seed beads and 4mm beads and a delicate glass teardrop in the center.

This textured, vintage-looking piece combines multiple layered and colored filigrees, wire beaded edges, and beaded flowers to make an elaborate pendant necklace.

OTHER STRINGING MATERIALS:
Basic Knotted Bracelet

Knotted pearls are classic. While separating and defining the beads, knotting prevents the pearls from sliding off should the strand break. There are various techniques and stringing materials available for making a knotted bead strand. For this two-tone glass pearl bracelet, you will use a bead knotting tool and nylon beading thread. The bracelet ends are finished with clamshells, which are easily strung on and folded over for quick completion.

WHAT YOU'LL LEARN . . . .

- How to use beading thread and a beading needle
- How to use a clamshell end for beading
- How to use a knotting tool for consistent knots

WHAT YOU'LL NEED . . . .

TOOLS

- Scissors
- Big eye beading needle
- Knotting tool
- Chain-nose pliers
- Ruler

MATERIALS

- 32" (81.5 cm) nylon beading thread: size 2, gold

- Ten 8mm glass pearls: gold
- Nine 8mm glass pearls: ivory
- Two gold-tone clamshell ends with attachment loops
- One 4.5mm gold-tone jump ring (22 gauge)
- One 6mm gold-tone jump ring (20 gauge)
- One 12mm gold-tone lobster clasp
- G-S Hypo Cement glue (optional)

How to Make a Basic Knotted Bracelet

1 Cut a piece of *thread* four times the length of the bracelet you are making. Thread it through the big eye needle, bringing the ends of the thread together. Tie an overhand knot at the end of the two strands. Enlarge the knot by tying a second overhand knot over the first one. Slide on a clamshell end to cover the knot.

2 Slide on one 8mm gold glass pearl. With your left hand, if you are right-handed, make a "V" with your index and middle finger. The middle finger should be closer to your palm. Holding the end of the thread with your right hand, wrap the thread away from you around your index finger and then your middle finger and bring it around to the side facing you. Drop the pearl over the wrapped thread into the loop you have formed around your fingers.

3 Point the tip of the awl on the knotting tool through the loop from left to right and wrap the thread halfway around it.

4 Slide the thread loop off of your fingers onto the awl portion of the knotting tool.

QUICK REFERENCE

Thread. The most common stringing materials are nylon thread and silk thread. Nylon is very durable, and silk hangs nicely and comes in a wide variety of colors. You can get prethreaded cards of either material, or you can use a beading needle and a spool of beading thread. Whether you are working with a single or a double strand of thread, it is important that you select the correct thickness for the style of beading you are doing, especially if you are knotting. If your thread is too thin, the knot will slide through the bead, and if your thread is too thick, you may not be able to get it pulled through the bead on a needle when it is doubled over. Beading thread, especially silk, may need to be stretched before using, as larger beads will cause the thread to stretch over time. You may wish to coat your thread with beeswax before stringing to make stringing and knotting easier. Needles come in several styles as well, so choose one that suits the beading cord you are using.

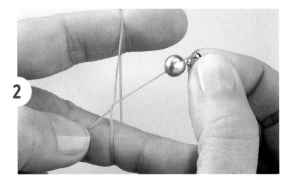

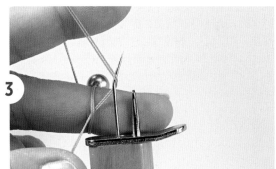

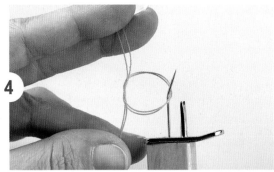

5 Pull the thread so that it tightens around the awl and also so that the knot slides toward the pearl.

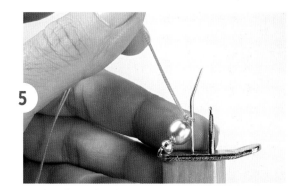

6 Turn the tool in your right hand, reversing the position of the awl and Y prong. Place the thread into the Y prong and pull the thread tight. Keep your left index finger on the top portion of the awl so that the thread does not slide off the tip until you want it to. Carefully slide the knot toward the top of the awl, and onto the bent tip. Keeping the tension in the thread through the Y prong, use your right thumb to push up on the spring-loaded metal top of the tool. This will slide the knot off of the awl and tighten the knot next to the pearl. Slide an ivory 8mm pearl onto the thread, and repeat the knotting technique. Keep adding pearls and knotting, alternating the gold and ivory, until you have added ten gold pearls and nine ivory pearls.

7 Make a knot after the last pearl. Slide on the second clamshell with the shell portion facing away from the beads. Use the knotting tool to make a knot inside the clamshell, and then repeat a second time.

8 Trim excess thread and use chain nose pliers to close the clamshell. Bend the end prong into a closed loop. Close the clamshell on the other end of the bracelet and make a loop. Hook the 4.5mm jump ring and clasp to one clamshell loop and close the jump ring. Open the 6mm jump ring and attach it to the other clamshell loop. Close the jump ring.

TIP For extra security, put a touch of glue on the end knots before closing the clamshell ends.

Variations

Put a new spin on the classic knotted pearl bracelet by alternating pearls with faceted glass beads and varying the bead sizes.

These delicate hoop earrings are constructed like miniature bracelets, only using one clamshell end on each.

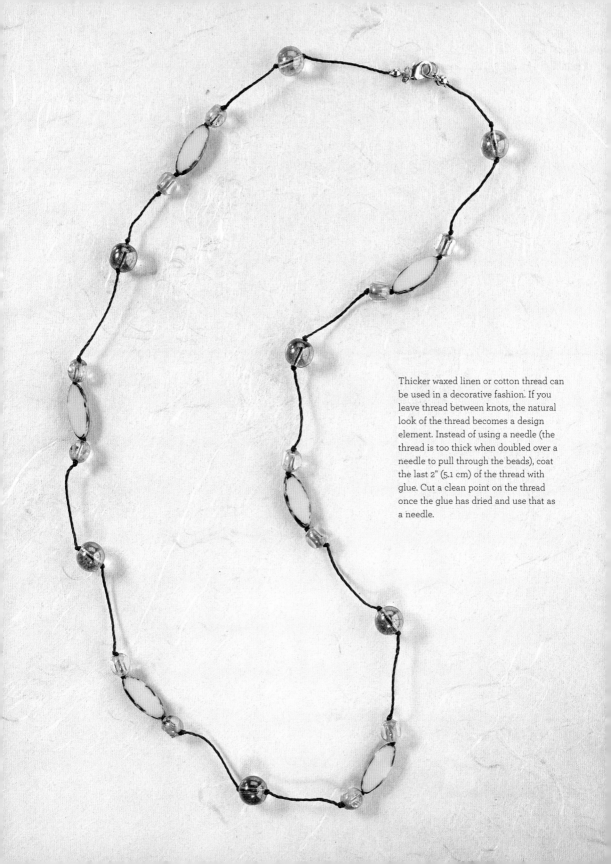

Thicker waxed linen or cotton thread can be used in a decorative fashion. If you leave thread between knots, the natural look of the thread becomes a design element. Instead of using a needle (the thread is too thick when doubled over a needle to pull through the beads), coat the last 2" (5.1 cm) of the thread with glue. Cut a clean point on the thread once the glue has dried and use that as a needle.

OTHER STRINGING MATERIALS:
Elastic Bracelet

Beading elastic is a UV resistant stretch cord specifically designed for beaded jewelry applications. Stretch cord allows you to bead bracelets that do not require a clasp and can be slipped on and off the wrist by stretching over the hand. It is available in a number of diameters from .8mm to .1mm. You will use the .8mm for this project; it is small enough to fit through the holes in most beads, but still strong enough to maintain its stretch for an extended period of time.

WHAT YOU'LL LEARN . . . .

- How to use beading elastic
- How to finish elastic designs
- How to use spacer beads to give the design more interest

WHAT YOU'LL NEED . . . .

TOOLS

- Scissors
- Ruler

MATERIALS

- 11" (27.9 cm) .8mm beading elastic
- Eight 4 × 10mm blue tube beads
- Eight 4 × 6mm flat metallic spacer beads
- Eight 8mm oval flat beads: brown tiger AB
- G-S Hypo Cement glue

How to Make an Elastic Bracelet

TIP Some types of beads are not recommended for use with elastic. Crystal beads and heavy base metal beads can wear through the elastic, causing it to break. The metallic spacers used in this project are lightweight metallized plastic. Small diameter cord can also be at risk for breakage.

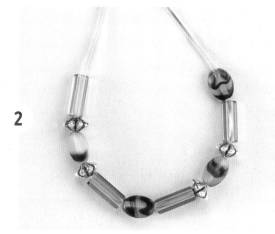

1 Cut 11" (27.9 cm) of beading elastic. Slide on one blue tube bead followed by a silver spacer, a brown oval, and another silver spacer. Continue by adding another blue tube, a brown oval and a third blue tube.

2 Continue the pattern, adding a spacer, a brown oval, and another spacer. Continue with a blue tube, followed by a brown oval. This is the halfway point of the bracelet. Finish the bracelet by repeating the exact same pattern.

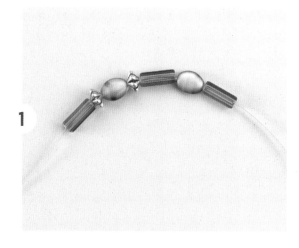

3 Once all of the beads are on the bracelet, hold one end of the elastic in each hand. Wrap the left-hand side twice around the right-hand side and then wrap the right-hand side back once around the left side forming a knot. The two ends can be tied together one more time for extra security. Dab a drop of G-S Hypo Cement glue onto the knot and allow it to dry. Trim the excess elastic ends.

TIP Using large diameter elastic may create a very large knot when the elastic is tied off. These knots can be hidden inside of a bead with an oversized hole. Using smaller diameter elastic avoids the large knot issue.

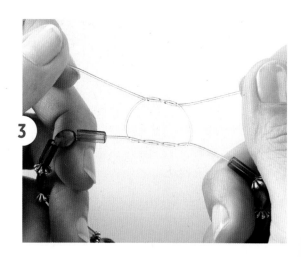

Variations

This bracelet is designed using larger metallized plastic beads. It is sized slightly larger to be worn more like a cuff.

Elastic cord can also be used to make rings. This ring is made using an elephant bead and e-beads.

Another great use for elastic is watchbands. Watchbands can be fairly short so that the band fits snugly around the wrist and the watch face stays on top of the wrist. This leafy band was constructed using two strands of elastic.

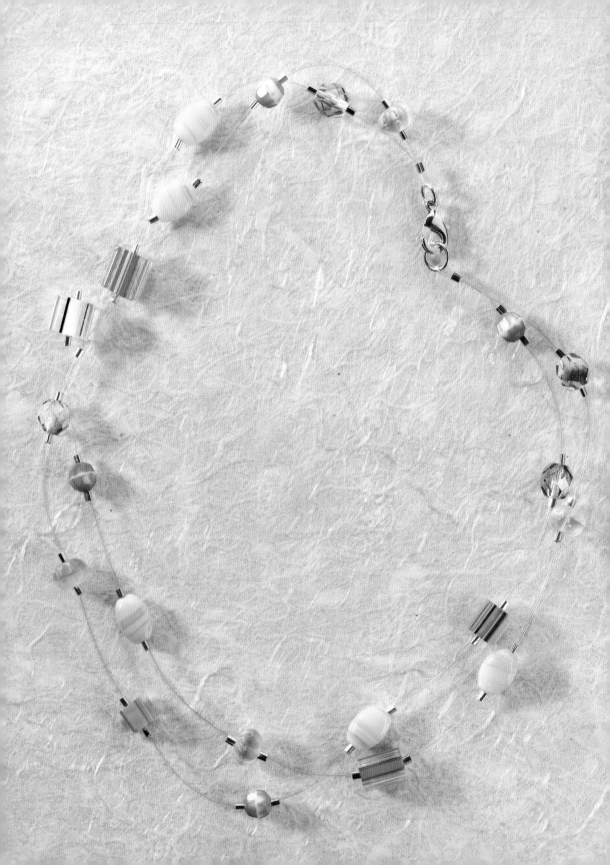

OTHER STRINGING MATERIALS:
Two-Strand Illusion Necklace

Monofilament is similar to fishing line, but there is a supple, durable version made for jewelry. The clear filament gives the illusion that the beads are floating on air, which is ideal for highlighting glass beads, like the multicolor striped furnace beads that accent this double strand project. Since a single-strand necklace on monofilament is so delicate, it is nice to combine two or more strands for more impact, while still maintaining the floating appearance of the beads.

WHAT YOU'LL LEARN

- How to mark bead placement on monofilament
- How to crimp beads in place
- How to offset two illusion strands for maximum impact

WHAT YOU'LL NEED

TOOLS

- Crimp pliers
- Chain-nose pliers
- Wire cutters
- Fine-point permanent marker
- Ruler

MATERIALS

- 40" (101.6 cm) clear monofilament nylon line: .016" diameter
- Four 6 × 8mm pumpkin-shaped pressed glass beads: bright yellow-green matte AB (ghost)
- Four 6mm pressed glass round faceted beads: opaque orange and white
- Four 6 × 8mm pressed glass oval beads: opaque yellow stripe
- One 8 × 8mm square furnace bead: white stripe
- Two 8 × 10mm square furnace beads: orange stripe
- One 6 × 7mm triangle furnace bead: yellow stripe
- One 6 × 6mm square furnace bead: green stripe
- Four 6mm Czech fire-polished beads: clear with rust luster coating
- Forty-six 2mm gold-tone crimp tubes
- One 4.5mm gold-tone jump ring (22 gauge)
- One 12mm gold-tone lobster claw clasp
- One 6mm gold-tone jump ring (20 gauge)

How to Make a Two Strand Illusion Necklace

1 For a 16" (40.6 cm) necklace, cut two 20" (50.8 cm) pieces of monofilament. Using the permanent marker, mark the center of the first piece with a small dot. Make five more dots on each side of the center mark 1¼" (3.2 cm) apart, for a total of eleven dots. Repeat for the second piece.

2 Crimp a tube over the first dot at one end of one strand. Slide on a pumpkin bead and then another crimp tube. Crimp the tube next to the bead. The crimps will hold the bead in place and hide the pen mark. Continue to crimp beads in place in the following order: orange and white faceted bead, yellow oval bead, white stripe furnace bead, orange and white 6mm bead, yellow oval bead, pumpkin bead, orange stripe **furnace bead**, yellow oval bead, pumpkin bead, Czech fire-polished bead.

Crimp the beads on the second strand in the following order: Czech fire-polished bead, yellow oval bead, orange stripe furnace bead, Czech fire-polished bead, pumpkin bead, yellow stripe furnace bead, orange and white 6mm bead, yellow oval bead, green stripe furnace bead, Czech fire-polished bead, orange and white 6mm bead.

3 Open the 4.5mm jump ring, add the the clasp, and close the jump ring. Slide the end of the first strand that starts with the yellow-green bead through a crimp tube. Slide the end of the second strand that starts with the fire-polished bead through the same crimp tube. Adjust the lengths of the two lines so that the yellow-green bead sits ½" (1.3 cm) from the crimp tube, and the fire-polished bead sits 1" (2.5 cm) from the crimp tube. Loop both strands through the jump ring attached to the clasp and back through the crimp tube. Adjust the loop size, crimp the tube, and trim off the excess line.

TIP By staggering the bead placement between strands, the beads will be easier to see, and will not overlap.

4 Close the 6mm jump ring. Slide a crimp bead onto the free ends of the beadedstrands. Make sure the strands are the same length. Loop the strand ends through the jump ring, and back through the crimp tube. Adjust the loop, crimp, and trim excess line.

Variations

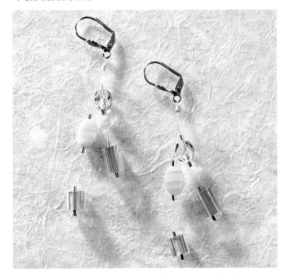

Make a coordinating pair of earrings by crimping beads onto two strands of monofilament, cutting the excess line on the end of the strands next to the crimp tube. Like the necklace, the two strands are staggered for maximum impact.

This bracelet only needs two crimp tubes. The stone chip beads are strung loosely on two separate strands, and then brought together periodically by a round stone bead.

This antique silver flower necklace expands on the idea of floating elements. The flowers are on a single strand illusion necklace. While adding each of the five center flowers, another piece of monofilament is looped through the bead on the necklace before it is crimped in place. Two large flowers are added to the ends of the looped pieces, and a small flower floats on the loop.

QUICK REFERENCE

Furnace beads, like many hand-made glass beads, have hole sizes that vary. Select beads with holes that won't slide over a crimped tube, which is 2mm or less.

RECYCLE, REUSE, AND REPURPOSE:
Recycled Bead Drop Earrings

Broken jewelry is an excellent source of beads and findings for your jewelry creations. There is nothing more fun than searching flea markets and yard sales for new treasures to design with. Not only can you find beads that are no longer on the market, you will be reusing pieces that otherwise may end up in the trash. Multistrand necklaces from the 1950s and 1960s are a great source of beads; look for interesting shapes, colors, and textures. Do not overlook plastic beads—they are lightweight and can be embellished with caps and spacers. This project shows how a couple of broken pieces can inspire many new styles.

WHAT YOU'LL LEARN..

- How to make new jewelry out of old
- How to combine different broken pieces
- How to make variations from the same broken piece

WHAT YOU'LL NEED..

TOOLS

- Chain-nose pliers
- Wire cutters

MATERIALS

- Broken jewelry, two different pieces
- Two 1" (2.5 cm) gold-tone headpins
- Two gold-tone lever-back wires

How to Make Recycled Bead Drop Earrings

1 Remove two coral beads, two bead caps, and two seed bead glass spacers from one of the broken pieces of jewelry.

TIP The coral colored necklace used for this project is part of what was a multistrand necklace from the 1950s. Parts from the same necklace were used for all of the variations in this project to give you an idea of the different looks that can be created from the same original piece.

2 Remove two long beads from the broken segmented necklace. In this case, the beads are already on eye pins; if you are working with beads that are not already on eye pins, slide each bead onto an eye pin and form a loop on the other end.

3 Slide each of the coral beads from the first broken necklace onto a gold-tone headpin and add a cap and a small glass bead above each. Make a loop in the headpin, trim any excess with the wire cutters.

4 Hook the loops at the top of the coral bead drops into the loop in the eye pin on the bottom of the long beads. Attach the top loop of the long beads onto a lever-back wire.

2

3

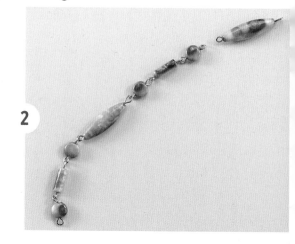

4

1

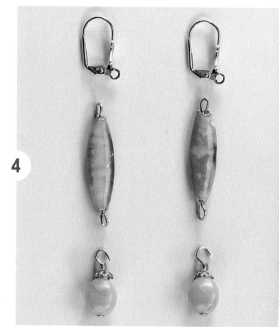

Variations

This summery bracelet is beaded using the coral beads from the original broken necklace as well as a few beads from a broken green necklace. The caps and the spacers give the bracelet an antique look.

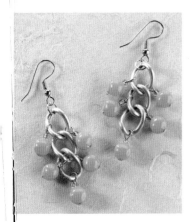

These modern earrings are made using two pieces of broken chain hung with five bead drops made from the original broken piece.

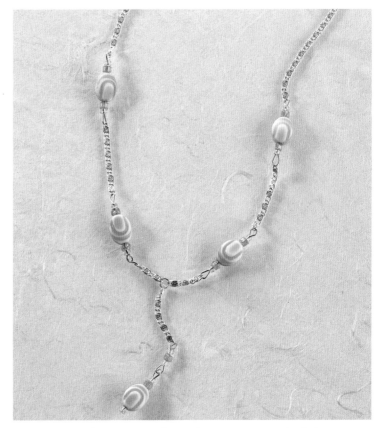

This "Y" style necklace is constructed using the interesting orange beads that were part of the original broken piece combined with bits of aluminum chain from another flea market find.

RECYCLE, REUSE, AND REPURPOSE:
Reuse Bracelet

While you are out looking for broken jewelry to enhance your designs, keep an eye out for other metal parts that can be used in jewelry. In this project you will create a bracelet by reusing metal disks that were part of a metal belt. Metal findings or parts can often be reassembled in different ways to form necklaces, pendants, bracelets, or earrings. They can be enhanced with added bead drops or combined with other metal parts. Look for interesting parts that have well-placed openings on which to add drops. The possibilities to create new jewelry by reusing metal parts are endless.

WHAT YOU'LL LEARN..

- How to reuse metal belt pieces
- How to combine metal disks with beads
- How to make variations from the same metal disks

WHAT YOU'LL NEED..

TOOLS

- Chain-nose pliers
- Wire cutters

MATERIALS

- Three 1½" (3.8 cm) metal disks from a broken belt
- Eight 12 to 14mm shaped faux pearls from a broken piece of jewelry

- Eight 1½" (3.8 cm) gold-tone eye pins
- One 12mm gold-tone lobster clasp
- Four 4mm gold-tone jump rings (22 gauge)
- Fourteen 6.5mm gold-tone jump rings (20 gauge)

How to Make a Reuse Bracelet

1 Remove eight faux pearls from a broken strand.

TIP In order to make a bracelet of the correct length for you, measure the size of the metal disks (the ones in this project are 1½" [3.8 cm]) and then vary the size of the connecting beads to change the length of the bracelet. See page 31 for the information on measuring bracelet length.

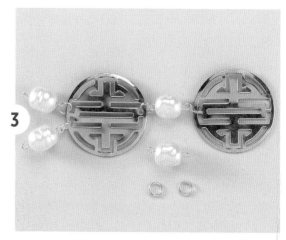

2 Place each of the pearls on an eye pin and form a loop on the end opposite the eye. Trim the excess and close the loop.

3 Use a 6.5mm jump ring to attach one end of a pearl segment to one of the metal disks. Attach the other end to another disk. Place two pearls between each of the three disks and then attach two pearls onto the disk at each end.

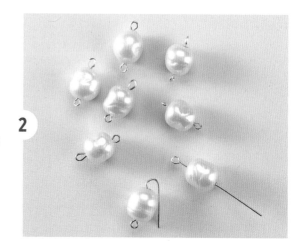

4 Once all of the pearl segments have been attached to the disks, attach one 4mm jump ring to each of the four pearl segments at the ends of the bracelet. At one end attach a 6.5mm jump ring through the two 4mm jump rings. At the opposite end attach a clasp on a 6.5mm jump ring through the two 4mm jump rings.

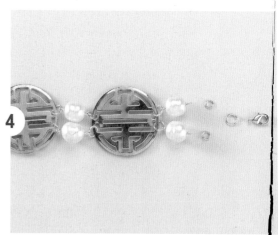

Variations

A variation of the project bracelet could be to use only one of the metal disks and then complete it by attaching two recycled blue bead segments and an assortment of recycled chain onto each side of the disk. The chain does not necessarily need to come from the same recycled broken piece; in fact the bracelet will be more interesting if multiple chain varieties are used.

These disk earrings are made by using three gold jump rings at the top and bottom of the disk to form an attachment. An earring finding is attached at the top and recycled crystal is used for the drop.

This necklace enhances the Asian feel of the gold disks. A single disk is combined with a recycled necklace that has rose quartz segments on it. The segment and chain combination are used as both the drops and the chain for the pendant.

RECYCLE, REUSE, AND REPURPOSE: Repurposed Necklace

Consider other household items made of beads that could be repurposed into jewelry designs. We disassembled a bamboo-bead placemat and combined the beads with an interesting assortment of broken jewelry beads to make a truly recycled piece. Do not be afraid to combine unusual beads and colors; this project combines the bamboo beads of the placemat with seed, nut, and wood beads from two different broken pieces and crackle purple plastic beads from a design that was probably made in the 1980s. This project is a recycled variation of the long beaded necklace on page 105.

WHAT YOU'LL LEARN..

- How to repurpose beads from other beaded household pieces
- How to combine repurposed beads with other recycled beads
- How to make variations from the same beads

WHAT YOU'LL NEED..

TOOLS

- Crimp pliers
- Wire cutters
- Ruler

MATERIALS

- 38" (96.5 cm) beading cable: .015", 49 strands

- Bamboo beaded placemat or other repurposed beads
- Broken jewelry, three different pieces
- Two 2mm silver-tone crimp tubes
- One 12mm silver-tone lobster clasp
- One 4mm silver-tone jump ring (22 gauge)
- One 6.5mm silver-tone jump ring (20 gauge)

How to Make a Repurposed Necklace

1 Dismantle the placemat and remove the beads that you will need for a long necklace.

TIP When working with placemats, you have the option of cutting up the entire piece right away and storing the beads in a resealable bag or storage container or simply cutting off the beads you are going to use for this project and then storing the placemats stacked on a shelf.

2 Slide the focal bead, in this case the purple plastic bead, onto the center of the beading cable. Starting in the center of the necklace helps you keep the design symmetrical. In this piece the flat natural seed beads are used as spacers. Slide three seed beads on each side of the purple bead followed by three small wood beads. Follow these with three more spacers, the placemat bamboo bead, three more spacers, three more wood beads, and three more spacers.

3 Follow the previous three spacers with a nut bead, then add three more spacers, three wood beads, three spacers, a bamboo bead, three spacers, three wood beads, and three more spacers. This completes the basic pattern. Follow this pattern on each side of the necklace two more times to finish the beading. Using the crimp tubes, finish the necklace by adding a loop on one end and a clasp on the other. Refer to page 99, steps 5 and 6.

Variations

This multistrand bracelet is designed using the necklace end findings from the broken coral necklace used for the Recycled Drop Earrings on page 179. The bamboo placemat beads are used in combination with brass and wood beads from another piece of broken jewelry.

These fun hoop earrings were constructed from loops salvaged from a broken piece combined with drops made from the bamboo placemat beads and other recycled wood beads.

This chain and bead necklace uses the bamboo beads in combination with some of the black beads that were on the 1980s necklace and assorted recycled wood beads and recycled chain. Again, a completely different look can be achieved using elements from just a f ew broken pieces of jewelry.

Resources

Jewelry Supplies

Artbeads
Web site: www.artbeads.com

Beadalon
Web site: www.beadalon.com

Fire Mountain Gems and Beads
Web site: www.firemountaingems.com

Hidden Hollow Beads
Web site: www.hiddenhollowbeads.com

Land of Odds
Web site: www.landofodds.com

Michaels Stores
Web site: www.michaels.com

Rings and Things
Web site: www.rings-things.com

Rio Grande
Web site: www.riogrande.com

Shipwreck Beads
Web site: www.shipwreckbeads.com

South Pacific Wholesale Co.
Web site: www.beading.com

International Sources for Jewelry-Making Supplies

Beadfx
Web site: www.beadfx.com

The Bead Shop
Web site: www.beadshop.co.uk

Beads Unlimited
Web site: www.beadsunlimited.co.uk

Gems2Behold
Web site: www.gems2behold.com

Katie's Treasures
Web site: www.katiestreasures.com.au

Space Trader
Web site: www.spacetrader.com.au

Dedication

We dedicate this book to two wonderful men: Ai Buangsuwon, Ann's husband, and Randy Townsend, Karen's husband. We cherish your love and support.

Acknowledgments

We would like to express our appreciation for the support and generosity of the following people and company:

- Our mother, Annamarie Mitchell
- Ann's kids, Mitch and Alex Buangsuwon
- Our favorite bead guy, Tony Masso
- Thank you to all of our dedicated customers who have supported us for years.

Beading wires, tools and many of the findings supplied by Beadalon. www.beadalon.com; (866) 423-2325

About the Authors

Sisters Ann and Karen Mitchell started their mixed media jewelry business, AnKara Designs, in 1991. Together, they authored the book *Liquid Polymer Clay: Fabulous New Techniques for Making Jewelry and Home Accents* (Krause Publications). They also add to their credits experience as teachers, columnists, and craft product designers. The duo has made numerous guest appearances on television including The Carol Duvall Show, DIY Jewelry Making, and DIY Craft Lab. Their delicate, feminine jewelry design style and innovative ideas have appeared in feature films, television, theatre, museum exhibitions, advertisements, websites, books, and magazines.

Index